P9-CED-460

DISCARD

Friendship

Contents

Acknowledgments

THOSE TO WHOM I OWE THE MOST are the survey respondents. They gave generously of their time and permitted me, a stranger, briefly to enter their personal lives.

Gail Block, my wife, has again served as my on-site, instantly responsive editor, sounding board, and, above all, friend.

Stacy Winslow has been more than a typist, critic (always right!) and enthusiastic supporter. She, too, has been a friend.

I am indebted to Marcia Cohen, who assisted with the celebrity interviews. And to Aaron Cohen, vice-president of sales, NBC, my gratitude.

My thanks to Lisa Collier, my literary agent, for her belief in the project.

Michael Tapes, with his technical expertise and consideration, rescued me when I found some of my recorded interviews to be barely audible.

x • Acknowledgments

The librarians at the Half Hollow Hills Library in Dix Hills, New York, were resourceful, gracious and kind.

Finally, my appreciation is extended to the many research assistants who helped distribute the questionnaire.

Author's Note

WITH THE EXCEPTION of the celebrities interviewed, the privacy of the people described herein was protected by altering names and other insignificant external characteristics; the essential psychological and social dynamics involved have been preserved. Any resemblance to real persons is strictly intentional; any identification with particular persons is, I trust, impossible.

Friendship

Introduction

SEVERAL YEARS AGO, a vivid and disturbing dream of a friend's death in an auto accident broke my sleep. The friend—alive and well as far as I know—was one of a group of close intimates I hadn't seen for a decade, since my graduate-school years. I was so shaken by the imagery of my friend's demise and puzzled by the meaning of the dream that I didn't want to return to sleep. I needed to make sense of this thing. A few hours later, weary but restless, it dawned on me that I had just said goodbye to an era, to close friends with whom I had lost touch. It was a violent ending; apparently, letting go was not easy. These were people and times that had meant a lot to me.

Before this incident, I hadn't given much thought to the undercurrent of friendship in my life. As most of us do, I had taken the friendship experience for granted. That dream and the curi-

1

osity it engendered were to be the inspiration for a long and exciting journey into the unexplored terrain of the friendship landscape.

Friendship is an untapped natural resource. Particularly during the difficult times of recent years—high unemployment and inflation, a loss of faith in government and a general disenchantment with traditional values—friends can offer comfort and support; they are the threads keeping us connected to the world. The evidence is all around us that friendship is valued. Making sure that children have friends is a fundamental parenting function; the lure of "friendship" is used to sell successfully almost anything—from real estate to deodorant; Dale Carnegie's book *How To Win Friends and Influence People*, written in 1936, is still a hot item after ninety-five printings and almost eight million copies sold.

It is not that Carnegie's popular book fulfills the promise of its title; it doesn't. It is yet another con—an assemblage of emotional scraps—foisted upon a society hungering for friendship. That it remains everlastingly in print attests to our unsatisfied appetite.

Some social scientists report that the desire for friendship and discussions about loneliness have replaced sex as the number-one topic on college campuses. In fact, much of the social activity of individuals today can be described as search behavior; moving to new cities, beginning new jobs, changing marital partners leads us, sometimes frantically, to seek replacements for those friends who either are no longer present or who no longer share the same interests.

Despite our longing for friendship, it isn't always easy to achieve or sustain; there are few guiding rules in conducting friendships and the paradoxes don't help any. We spill our most personal secrets to a stranger, yet we ignore the misfortune of an old friend because we are uneasy about reestablishing the former intimacy. We put off seeing a friend and reunite with a vague sense of dread only to find the experience surprisingly joyous. A friend of long standing calls in trouble and we no longer have the desire to help; a new friend calls and we offer everything. We rarely think of older people as potential friends; younger ones are similarly ruled ineligible. And should a friend become unusually successful, a strain is immediately placed on the relationship. We are both driven toward friendship and repelled from it by the complexities of our personalities.

Some of us think of friends as people to spend time with when there isn't anything better to do. Those of us taking this position complain of a sense of loneliness, yet friendship is deferred to the pursuit of self-absorption. In these instances, the careful tending required of friendship yields to the likes of EST, Actualization and Yoga.

It is a mistake to assume that individual growth can take precedence over relationships; the effort ceases to be growth because we cannot expand without involvement outside ourselves. We learn in friendship to look with the eyes of another person, to listen with another's ears and to feel with another's heart. If a child grows up without comrades, he or she does not develop an ability to identify with other people. This is the child who as an adult has difficulty considering the needs of others. Friendship is training for living in a social world.

Considering the importance of friendship, it comes as a surprise that it has largely been ignored by social scientists. There has been a plethora of books on man-woman relationships and the parent-child dilemma. Our society informs us of the behavior of husbands and wives and the obligations binding parents and children. Other human attachments, the sexual union, the family, the group have been the objects of intensive study. Only a handful of human-relations professionals even mention friendship in their writings. The theme has been left to poets and novelists. It is as though those in the psychological profession assume that, unlike other relationships, friendship happens of its own accord and consequently the quality and frequency of friendship experiences is beyond our direct control. Friendship remains the one vast, fertile area of human living that is unexplored. The friendship experience has been orphaned.

As a psychologist, I am no more immune to loneliness than anyone else. Frustrations with friendship have unsettled me as they may have you. Prompted by a dream, this book, filled with the wisdoms, failings and rich experiences of nearly two thousand people who kindly lent themselves to the research effort, is an attempt to take our friendship temperature, to see through real-life people what friendship is like in America. Although no pat answers, no ready-made formulas will be prescribed, trends that offer direction will become apparent. Looking at the friendship patterns we have individually and collectively formed will, I hope, provide a long overdue roadmap for the dilemmas and emotional joys of the friendship journey.

About the Survey

THERE IS AN ELECTRICITY about friendship relationships; they are like no other. Though we might not be able to choose our neighbors, relatives or the people with whom we work, friendships are an act of pure intention. Very few associations allow for such a free exchange of loyalty, trust, affection and, sometimes, doubt, hurt and anger. Friendship not only begins on a voluntary basis, but it continues by choice. The depth and rhythm of the relationship, the desire and willingness to respond to each other are open to negotiation. The process of choice may not be quick nor may it develop spectacularly—the yearning for a good friend is frequently frustrated—but make no mistake about it, most of us are involved in the search: Friendship matters.

Beginning when we learn to walk, the hunger for friendship weaves its way into our consciousness. The feelings we develop for one another beyond sex and the family—those complex and essential connections we call friendship—tend to make life more exciting; whether or not they satisfy, produce conflict, destroy or uncover a new dimension of personality, they certainly intensify our existence. Man, woman, married or unmarried, if you've ever been a friend, wanted a friend, lost a friend, loved a friend, the friendship experience is likely to be a recurring theme in your life:

"From junior high school through high school my close friends were mainly girls. I had a special friend whom I walked arm in arm with; we confided in each other and faithfully held one another's secrets in confidence. Life at that time seemed full of secrets: the secret of pubic hair, of wanting to defy mother and, of course, the big secret of sexual relations. But after junior high school, I stopped having one special girlfriend in whom I confided. In fact, by the time I was fifteen I didn't discuss my personal feelings with anyone. I no longer had close friends. I remember, in spite of all my girlfriends, feeling lonely, as if the surrounding world was hostile and impersonal.

"When I was about seventeen, I started to date. This is when friendship was replaced by the dream of Prince Charming. Occasionally I even dared talk about my Prince Charming fantasies with other girls, but our conversations were guarded; there was an underlying rivalry between us. We became more and more private. This saddened me because I had begun to miss the closeness of friends. I was really mystified by the whole dating process and wanted very much to talk to someone about my feelings. It was very frustrating because other girls seemed very unwilling. It was always a case of, 'Sure, I'd love to, if there isn't anything better to do.' This meant, 'as long as a boy doesn't call!' As much talk as there is about women's liberation, I'm still not satisfied with my relationships with other women. I've gotten hurt several times. Even with women I feel close to, I, as a woman, come second when a man comes on the scene. I have never recaptured the close feeling of friendship I had in junior high school."

*

"When I was twenty-nine, I had a miserable year. The woman I loved, my wife, was involved with another man. My friend Martin, older and wiser, listened patiently as I poured my heart out. He was there when I needed him; two in the morning or mid-afternoon, he listened and gave me advice. I told him of my suspicions and her denial. He encouraged me to believe her and trust her. Despite my efforts to look the other way, I was besieged with distress. I felt as if my life was falling apart—I would fantasize losing my family, my home, starting from scratch—and panic would set in. Knowing that Martin was there enabled me to survive. It was the first time I had ever relied so heavily on another man, a friend. He was like a rock in my life, very supportive. We ate together, talked well into the night on several occasions. We really drew very close. Just as I had calmed down and started to believe my wife, she confessed. I was right all along. I packed my things that night and left.

"After I was divorced, I found that Martin was once her lover. Betrayed isn't a strong enough word for how I felt. Knifed in the back is more like it. When I confronted Martin, he was open about it. He had not been her lover all along, he said, but had been lured into a brief affair by my tales of love toward her. That was six years ago. Martin is still married and I am still single. Owing more to our different life styles than to anger, I don't see Martin any longer, but occasionally I think of him. I don't blame him. I no longer feel betrayed. I know people would think I'm crazy—that he took advantage of my trust—but I feel he actually did help me and that his motives for comforting me were basically sincere—based on our friendship. If things became complicated that's because relationships are complex. How we feel about people and they about us is not a simple thing that fits a ready-made formula. I don't think most of us plan to hurt those we care about, but it happens. No, Martin wasn't a safe friend, but I learned from him. I feel wiser, and for that I am grateful."

*

"When Edward and I started to see each other, we pretty much cut ourselves off from friends. Evenings, weekends and holidays were spent in romantic isolation—long walks in the woods, drives down to the beach, dinner at his apartment or mine, just the two of us together. We kept in touch with our friends during the day by either phone or an occasional lunch. This went on for a few months and then gradually we ventured out with other couples; we started to open the doors to the dowry of friends each of us brought to the relationship. That we had remained single through our twenties is a factor here; we both had a fairly large circle of friends. Each time we merged there was excitement but also an underlying suspense and tension: Will he like my friends? Will they like him? What will his friends think of me? He'd known all his friends from childhood and, in my view, the only thing they had in common was a shared history. There were tremendous differences in interests, occupations and, sometimes, in values. I couldn't understand why he still clung to them and he couldn't understand why I was so critical. There was this one time when we went out to dinner with a friend of his and his wife and the whole night was spent talking about old times. I got stuck listening to this woman's child-care complaints and was bored to death. Oh, did I wish we had never come out of hiding that night!

"When I refused to spend time with his friends, he was not sympathetic. Matter of fact it caused quite a rift. It was as if I was rejecting him. I insisted I was marrying him, not his friends. He was in strong disagreement about this but compromised by seeing his friends without me. I've now decided it won't kill me to spend some time with people I don't particularly care for. I'm more tactful now and I try not to overreact. As I think back to the early part of our relationship, that seclusive phase, I'm glad we didn't rush out to inspect each other's world immediately. That time gave us a chance to solidify as a couple, to get to know each other better and form a good communication network before we moved into an area that turned out to be surprisingly sensitive. As it was, I had to reassure him that I wasn't pirating him away from his friends. We're married seven years now and we've both changed. The friendships he forms now are much more to my liking and his old friends, who think he's the salt of the earth, no longer see me as strange. I'm even fairly close to some of them and he has developed some close ties with my friends."

Friends, pals, buddies, chums, comrades, sisters, brothers—the names we give our nonrelated intimates are not critical. Men and men, women and women, and women and men—the human condition "wires" us with a basic desire to make contact. *That* is critical. When friendship works, it is an emotional celebration. We establish and maintain friendships with the hope they will enrich our existence. Friends join us in a kind of conspiracy against the world; we and our friends like one another, share interests, have similar life styles or similar problems in living.

It is with our friends that we stand the best chance of being truly ourselves. The friendship bond is unique. Although friendships, like romantic ties, are often entangled with competition, jealousy and betrayal, they tend to offer more psychological space than other attachments. Friendship is open ended; unlike family and mate relations, we and our friends live separate lives, allowing time off from the fray and, consequently, a greater tolerance for change and growth.

It is indisputable that friendship can become one of life's deepest pleasures. Indeed, in our personal, disconnected society, friends may be more a necessity than a luxury; they form the backdrop against which we play out our professional, sexual and familial lives. To put the matter more bluntly, in the modern world friendships are not optional. Whether it is our basic need for a feeling of community with others, a need to relate with a few intimates, or a desire to confirm and expand our ideas, values and beliefs, most of us welcome the support of a network, a lifeline of friends. Yes, friendship matters.

Friendship is a contemporary portrait of those ties—not

primarily blood or marriage related—that play a special part in our lives; it is a hunt for answers—the questions pertain to our friends and ourselves—and an exploration of the everyday and not-so-everyday struggles each of us has in our efforts to make emotional connections with others. It is an examination in intimate detail of the friendship patterns in America—the manifold ways in which friendships affect and contribute to our lives —and a critical appraisal of the prevailing myths.

Friendship. The power of the word leads to widely varied and hotly contested notions of what friendship is; how friendships are conducted by people of the same sex; whether or not friendships can really exist between the sexes; how marriage and divorce affect friendships; how friendships affect marriage and divorce and much more. To go beyond popular myths, to study the customs, problems and real-life friendship experiences in our society, an intensive research program was launched.

This book is the end product of that effort. It is based on roughly five hundred interviews, many of them in depth, the available social-science literature (of which there is an astonishing paucity) and a national questionnaire survey distributed personally at vacation resorts, busy shopping centers and through mass mailings. The survey was completed by 2,063 people whose demographics—age, sex, marital status, religious and educational backgrounds, geographic location, socioeconomic position—were reasonably representative of the American middle class.

The questionnaire was concise but detailed; it contained multiple-choice items as well as an optional open-ended question that allowed for an essay-type response. Many individuals wrote lengthy replies to this question and voluntarily contributed additional dimensions of their friendship experience. This correspondence, along with the supplemental interviews, is the source of the numerous first-person statements in the text. To the best of my knowledge, this is the largest and most up-to-date body of information extant about friendship in our society.

While yielding definitive data has been an objective of this

Age

18–21	8%
22–29	23%
30–39	27%
40–44	11%
45–54	26%
55 and over	5%

Sex

Male	47%
Female	53%

Marital Status

Married	56%
Living together arrangement	3%
Single	24%
Separated/Divorced	14%
Widowed	3%

Children

About half of the respondents had children. Of these, 37% of the children were under 6 years of age and 48% were 6 or over but below 18. The remainder were 18 or older.

Religion

Protestant	42%
Catholic	24%
Jewish	12%
Other	12%
No formal religion	10%

Education

Some high school	8%
High school graduate	28%
Some college	29%
College graduate	20%
Some graduate school/ professional training	8%
Postgraduate degree	7%

Occupation

Professional	29%
Managerial	21%
Other white collar	16%
Blue collar	19%
Nonemployed (Homemaker, retired, student, out of work)	15%

Income Levels

Under $10,000	10%
$10,000–$14,999	9%
$15,000–$19,999	29%
$20,000–$24,999	30%
$25,000 and over	22%

City/County

Big city	48%
Small city	16%
Suburb	32%
Rural	4%

Geographic Location

Northeast	27%
Southeast	12%
Northwest	16%
West Coast	21%
Midwest	13%
Southwest	11%

project since its inception (the research was carried out over a three-year period beginning in late 1975) and it is intended to provide useful guidance, it is not a compilation of statistics, and not a "how-to" manual, but a book of human experiences. Data are given where numbers are particularly surprising, enlightening or fascinating, but in the main the significant findings of the survey are presented through and supported by the words of the respondents themselves. They are far more meaningful to most people than are tables, charts and graphs. The voices of our peers are certainly more colorful and persuasive than any statistic.

A heavy emphasis on very specific, step-by-step advice has been avoided because it is believed that such advice, freely dispensed to unknown individuals, is unrealistic. We humans are very complex; to fit our multifaceted emotional beings to one prescription or one form of friendship is to invite frustration. For the most part, we all have to puzzle out our own friendship solutions. I am not presumptuous enough to offer answers, but I did discover connections; despite the confusion and contradictions, certain patterns seemed to emerge. Myths were shattered. Current doctrines were challenged. These are valuable guideposts and are gladly shared.

Certainly there are some characteristics most of us desire from our friendships, such as companionship, trust and loyalty. We expect to enjoy our friends, to have a warm exchange with them and be respected by them. But even here the recipe for accomplishing these goals is individualistic. The care and nurturing of good friendship is ambiguous, the formula of ingredients uncertain. Honesty and good communication, yes, but baring our souls? Some nod affirmatively, others—though able to give and receive warmth—only fleetingly discuss intimacies with their friends. Still others—we have all encountered them—although willing to spill their life story in excruciating detail, maintain superficial relationships.

To define friendship becomes even more difficult. There is no magical standard of friendship fitting us all. People thrive on an assortment of relationships—casual relations, intimate relations, love relationships. Letters are written, "Dear Friend. . . ." There is the "Friend" you have at Chase Manhattan. Is friendship a business arrangement? Some use the term "my friend" loosely; it is bandied about with complete disregard of attachment. They drift about with others as easy riders, in shallow alliances. To these individuals, the distinction between an acquaintance and a friend is blurred.

Others, in pursuit of perfect loyalty, bestow the title of "friend" with excessive caution. They use the term as if it were an extravagantly rare commodity threatened with extinction by overuse. To these individuals the only friendships are the ideal, a friend is a friend all the way—total love, support and trust are ever present—or is not a friend at all. The very word friendship, they remind us, originated as a verb form meaning "to love" in ancient Teutonic tribal languages. It is not to be debased.

When we talk about a friend we may be speaking of a co-worker, a neighbor, a weekly tennis partner, a retail merchant, an ex-lover, one or both members of a couple, a mate, a relative, an old roommate or one of the hundreds of acquaintances that fill our lives. Friendships, I have found, are conducted at many levels of intensity, serve many different functions, meet different needs and range from casual to close in commitment. Consider the following varieties:

Convenience Friends. These are the people with whom we exchange favors—a next-door neighbor, a coworker, someone whose path we cross on a frequent basis. They will take care of your car and water your plants when you are on vacation. You will do the same for them. Seldom do convenience friends ever become close; the foundation of the relationship is lending a friendly hand, and if this factor should erode, the friendship may be allowed to fade.

Doing-Things Friends. These friends are also unlikely to be intimate. They are based on the sharing of mutual interests or activities. Into this group will fall the bowling-team members, associates in a service organization, fellow hobbyists.

Milestone Friends. These are friends in memory, who knew us when—the college roommate, former traveling companion, a person who shared high times or misfortune—and with whom we can talk about old times. Many of us imbue milestone friends with a romantic glow even though the years have gone by and we've little in common now. An exchange of holiday greetings, contact once a year or less, keeps these friendships—the embodiment of dreams and dramas now past—alive.

There are also *mentor friendships*—people who have been where we are and help us to make sense of it. There are part-of-a-couple friendships; the individuals are companionable, easy to talk to, but for some reason—lack of time or lack of chemistry—we don't usually see them alone. And there are good friends—people we feel especially close to, see often, can count on when we need them. It is with these individuals that we are apt to share much of our private lives, to celebrate our joys and obtain sustenance in a sometimes bleak world. A young woman expressed the meaning of this kind of friendship for her:

"There are friends I have grown up with and with whom I have shared important parts of my life—my memories, our home town, our youth. And then there are friends you meet later in life with whom you share more than a common history; with these friends there is a real exchange of thoughts and feelings. These are the people who will endure your ecstasies, who will fly with you. With these friends you are able to break down barriers, to go beyond common experience.

"When I am with such an exceptional companion, time stands still. It is for these people I reserve the glowing hours, too good not to share. I don't need cigarettes, food or liquor, I get caught up in the experience. We seem to be parts of the same mind. The next day and for several days I feel more energetic, very optimistic. The effort of sharing, of getting involved, leaves me with an increase in power."

Many kinds of friendships will be considered in the chapters to follow, but it is the experience and the dilemma of close friendships—those that allow us to be more open and spontaneous, more insightful, less bound by conformity and less hidden behind the masks of our existence—that were sought most ardently. They are the rarest find; all others, valuable as they may be, pale by comparison. In any case, tasting the flavor of a relationship, sensing its meaning, required more than a mass survey. To assure that the complexity of involvement was captured, one of every four respondents was contacted and many were interviewed at length.

In the final analysis, we are each the architects of our own friendships, choosing them and developing them in ways that suit our needs. Perhaps the best assistance a book such as this can offer is to describe honestly what is happening to friendship relationships today, and to depict how various kinds of people deal in various ways—some successfully, and some not—with the desire to be closer to other human beings. Sharing these experiences, the reader can judge where he or she stands—which forms of behavior to take as a model to live by, which to discard as useless and which, although enticing, may be tucked away for slow digestion and consideration at some future time.

Questioning Friendship

CONSIDERING THE COMPLEXITY of friendship relations, it would be ideal if there were some error-proof method to assess this behavior. Unfortunately, we cannot directly measure friendship behavior with special instruments or fancy electronic devices. Questionnaires have limitations, and interviews, although immensely supportive, do not provide a perfect resolution. People do not always tell the truth; they may sometimes distort reality either deliberately or because they are deceiving themselves.

Nonetheless, if we want to find out more about how we relate to each other, with all its problems the simple technique of asking is all we have, and that is what we must rely on. Happily, where the survey data could be compared with those obtained by other social scientists who have done research in this field, the results were reassuringly close; this adds confidence that the rest of the findings, which are not to be found elsewhere, are similarly trust-worthy. Additionally, more than half the survey respondents volunteered for an optional follow-up interview (either in person or by telephone) and, accordingly, included their names, addresses and telephone numbers. Such willingness to be scrutinized, to give up the anonymity of large-scale polls, allays suspicion of falsification.

Before judging what others say about friendship, consider some questions about friendship. These questions form the basis of the national survey and served as the foundation and major source for personal interviews. Most people frequently think about friendship—particularly in moments of loneliness—but few people give much thought to the elements that may go into friendship interactions, and that is what these questions try to do. Looking at and, if you wish, answering these questions will provide you with a framework within which to consider the answers others give.

The first ten questions covered basic personal information—household or marital status, geographic location, age, schooling, income, occupation, religion—and allowed for tabulation by background.

1. What is your age? _____

2. Sex: Male _____ Female _____

3. Family Income: What is the total income of your household before taxes? _____

4. What level of education do you have?
   Some high school   _____
   High school graduate   _____
   Some college   _____
   Some graduate training   _____
   Graduate degree   _____

5. Occupation (Include housewife or student):
    _____

6. Marital Status: Are you?
    Single   _____
    Married   _____
    Divorced   _____
    Widowed   _____
    Living with someone in a romantic-sexual
    relationship _____

7. How many children do you have?
    Under six years of age _____
    Over six years of age   _____

8. In what type of community do you live?
    Big city (one with a population of at least
    500,000)   _____
    Small city _____
    Suburb   _____
    Rural   _____

9. Where do you live?
    Northeast   _____
    Southeast   _____
    Northwest   _____
    West Coast _____
    Midwest   _____
    Southwest   _____

10. What is your religious background?
    Catholic   _____
    Protestant   _____
    Jewish   _____
    None of the above _____

Your Preteen Experiences (Ages 8–12)

11. Did you have friends as a child?
    Yes _____
    No _____

12. Did you feel liked, respected, accepted by other children?
    Yes _____
    No _____

13. Did you have a special, close friend during childhood?
    Yes _____
    No _____

14. If you did have a close friend was this person of the same or opposite sex?
    Same _____
    Opposite _____

Your Adolescent Experiences (Ages 13–18)

15. Did you feel liked, respected, accepted by others of your age?
    Yes _____
    No _____

16. Did you have a lot of friends?
    Yes _____
    No _____

17. Did you date?
    Frequently _____
    Moderately _____
    Not much _____
    Not at all _____

18. Did you have a special close friend of the same sex?

        Yes _____

        No _____

If so:

Was there a great deal of mutual trust?

        Yes _____

        No _____

Was there significant competition in the relationship?

        Yes _____

        No _____

Were you friends with this person as a preteenager?

        Yes _____

        No _____

Are you currently in touch with this person?

        Yes _____

        No _____

General Attitudes and Experiences (Adult Life)

19. What part would you like friendship to play in your life?

        Not important   _____

        Slightly important   _____

        Moderately important _____

        Very important   _____

20. Do you have a satisfactory circle of friendly acquaintances? (This might include neighbors, coworkers, recreational or sporting partners, fellow hobbyists and the like.)

        Yes _____

        No _____

21. We all differ somewhat in what we mean by "good friend." If this refers to a person, not kin, with whom you feel close,

talk personally, and on whom you can count, do you have a good friend of the same sex?

  Yes _____

  No _____

22. Do you have good friends of the opposite sex?

  Yes _____

  No _____

23. Which areas do you feel uneasy discussing personally with a good friend?

	Very Uneasy	*Uneasy*	*Feel Free*
Career ambitions	_____	_____	_____
Competition with others of the same sex	_____	_____	_____
Intimate sexual issues	_____	_____	_____
A problem in a love relationship	_____	_____	_____

24. Have you discussed the most difficult of the above issues with a friend during the past two years?

  Yes _____

  No _____

25. Would you prefer discussing the above issues with a person of the same sex or opposite sex?

  Same sex _____

  Opposite sex _____

  No preference _____

26. Would you like more male or female friends?

  Male _____

  Female _____

  Both _____

  Neither. I am not desirous of more friends. _____

27. I feel lonely:
     Never   _____
     Rarely   _____
     Sometimes   _____
     Often   _____

28. I feel depressed:
     Never   _____
     Rarely   _____
     Sometimes   _____
     Often   _____

29. In general, do you and your friends tend to be the same or similar in:

	Yes	No
Age	_____	_____
Level of schooling	_____	_____
Marital status	_____	_____
Income	_____	_____
Religious background	_____	_____

30. What have been the most crucial sources of dissatisfaction in your friendships with people of the same sex? (Check as many as apply.)
     We couldn't get personal   _____
     We didn't have time for
        each other   _____
     One of us became more
        successful than the other   _____
     Betrayal   _____
     Lack of candor   _____
     Competition   _____
     One of us felt the other
        was too critical   _____
     We found we had different
        interests   _____

We found we had different
values   _____
Other (indicate)   _____

31. Do you think friendships with people of the opposite sex
    are more difficult than friendships with people of the same
    sex?
        Yes   _____
        No   _____
    If so, in what ways are they more difficult? (Check as many
    as apply.)
        We have less in common   _____
        We have more difficulty
            understanding each other _____
        Sexual tensions complicate
            the relationship   _____
        Jealousy from my lover
            or mate creates problems _____
        Society views these friend-
            ships with suspicion _____
        Other (indicate)   _____

32. Have any of your past or current opposite-sex friendships
    included sexual involvement?
        Yes   _____
        No   _____
    If so, did the sexual involvement interfere with the friendship
    experience?
        Yes   _____
        No   _____

33. In your view, can friendship and sexual involvement be
    mixed?
        Yes   _____
        No   _____

34. What types of circumstances have you found most conducive to making friends?
    (Check as many as apply.)

Work	_____
School	_____
Neighbors, community	_____
Hobbies	_____
Organizations, social/ political causes	_____
Other (indicate)	_____

35. Do you consider yourself shy in social situations?

Yes	_____
No	_____

    If so, has shyness been a significant barrier to friendship?

Yes	_____
No	_____

36. From the list below, select *three* qualities you consider essential to close friendship:

Similarity in interests	_____
Trustworthy	_____
Mentally stimulating	_____
Accepting, nonjudgmental	_____
Emotionally open	_____
Responsive in a crisis	_____
Caring	_____
Independent	_____
Sense of humor	_____
Professionally accomplished	_____
Other (indicate)	_____

37. Of the characteristics below, which are most desirable in men? In women? Which are desirable in neither men nor

women? If you consider a characteristic desirable in men *and* women, check both.

	Men	Women	Neither
Assertive			
Independent			
Emotional			
Active			
Competitive			
Blunt			
Ambitious			
Tough			
Dominant			
Tender			
Expressive			
Sensitive			
Giving			
Aggressive			
Intelligent			

38. Which period of your life has been most productive of close friendships? Ages:

    20–25 _____
    25–30 _____
    30–35 _____
    35–40 _____
    40–50 _____
    50–60 _____

39. Does friendship seem to grow more important as you become older?

    Yes _____
    No _____

40. OPTIONAL: If you have ever had a good friend (of either sex), describe the relationship in detail. You might include

how you met, how long you have known each other, help-fulness in a time of crisis, disagreements, touching moments, and so on.

IF YOU HAVE NEVER BEEN MARRIED OR IN-VOLVED IN A LIVING-TOGETHER ARRANGE-MENT, STOP HERE.

Marriage and Friendship Experiences (for those living together over one year, consider yourselves married)

41. Do you consider your relationship fulfilling?
    Never   _____
    Rarely   _____
    Sometimes   _____
    Often   _____

42. What do you consider the *most* important aspect of a marital relationship?
    Sexual satisfaction   _____
    The opportunity to have
      children   _____
    Material things (accumula-
      tion of possessions)   _____
    Companionship (friendship) _____
    Someone to turn to
      in a crisis   _____
    Other (indicate)   _____

43. If you have children, do they contribute to you and your mate's feeling closer?
    Never   _____
    Rarely   _____
    Sometimes   _____
    Often   _____

44. Do you consider your mate to be a friend?

    Yes   _____

    No   _____

45. Do most of your friendship experiences primarily involve other couples?

    Yes   _____

    No   _____

46. In couples that you know, are you usually close friends with both partners or just one partner?

    Both   _____

    One partner   _____

    Neither   _____

47. If you are close with only one partner, do you see him or her separately on a regular basis?

    Yes   _____

    No   _____

    Does not apply   _____

Divorce and Friendship Experiences (for those currently or previously separated or divorced)

48. How long has it been since your initial separation?

    Less than one year   _____

    Between one and two years   _____

    Between two and three
    years   _____

    Over three years   _____

49. With whom did you discuss the details of your separation? (Check as many as apply.)

    A close married friend   _____

    Coworkers   _____

Family   _____
An unmarried friend   _____
A member of the clergy   _____
I did not discuss the divorce
    in detail with anyone   _____
Other (indicate)   _____

50. During the initial separation and divorce period, were your most active friendships the ones you developed with your mate during the marriage?

    Yes   _____
    No   _____

51. Did you develop new friends after your separation and divorce?

    Yes   _____
    No   _____

If so, how long was it before you found these new friends?

    Less than one year   _____
    Between one and two years _____
    Between two and three   _____
      years
    Over three years   _____

52. Do you consider your ex-spouse to be a friend?

    Yes   _____
    No   _____

Now, let's see what others have to say....

Sisterhood: Powerful or Treacherous?

A Code of Dishonor

WOMEN, AS THE STORY GOES, cannot be counted upon—for loyalty or for friendship. If friendship conflicts in any way with romantic interest in a man, then women, we are told, will ruthlessly sacrifice the bond of friendship. History does not celebrate female friendship as it does male camaraderie; rather it is filled with endless portrayals of women as each other's best enemies. Competing for men, from whom they derive their identity, they are depicted as fiercely—albeit subtly—rivalrous toward one another:

One evening at a party, Caroline went into one of the bedrooms to lie down for a few minutes. She swung open the door and stopped. Patricia, a friend for many years, and Walt, another friend's husband, were standing there talking. Their manner gave them away; standing so close and talking so seriously, it was clear that theirs was a romantic intimacy. Patricia knew the instant she saw Caroline's face in the doorway that her adventure had been discovered. Patricia couldn't be sure of Caroline's loyalty; the possibility existed that she might try to hurt her. She was frightened; if the affair were made public all hell would break loose. Some form of action had to be taken—and it was.

"At first Patricia stopped by to see me less frequently, then she didn't come by at all. Then, suddenly she was too busy to spend time with me when I dropped by her place. At first I really didn't notice the change. It may seem odd but I didn't connect what was happening to the party incident. To me, there was no point going into the details of that with Patricia. But when her avoidance of me finally registered, I challenged her. I asked if she felt awkward with me. She denied any uneasiness. Nothing was wrong, she said, 'I've just been busy.' In the coming months, a relationship I had thought of as supportive just stopped. Patricia never offered an explanation—and I didn't push any further. Patricia just wasn't the type to be pushed, she would only solidify her position and we would end up further apart.

"By the time summer rolled around, Patricia had cut me off completely. No phone calls, nothing. Then something else started to happen. I began to have a vague feeling of being an outsider among my own friends—mutual friends of Patricia and me. Then it hit me. The thought came like a jolt, while I was out for a walk by myself: Walt's wife was very suspicious; Patricia was terrified. An ingenious solution would be to find a target to deflect the suspicion. That was me! Since Walt's wife was already wary and not about to be soothed, at least Walt and Patricia could protect their relationship by offering me as a sacrifice. And if I went public with what I knew, who would believe me now? Patricia had spent months spreading rumors, laying the groundwork. I felt absolutely victimized. I was humiliated. How could I ever trust another woman again?

"Suddenly, little things that occurred over that year started to make sense. Comments that friends made—'Haven't seen you around your old haunts, keeping pretty busy?'—fell into place. I wondered why Uta, Walt's wife, snubbed me; I walked right by her, looked straight at her and said hello and she just stared through me. Intimacies with other friends had turned into polite social conversation. Now it all came together. I was a decoy in a vicious plan. It was a nightmare. I was terribly hurt. . . . After some months, with my feelings at least partially repaired, I moved out in search of new friends. I missed the daily intimacy and companionship of my old friends and was unsure that I would find it again, but I refused to have anything to do with them. As far as I was concerned, I had no friends left. Patricia saw to that; she made a clean sweep."

The contributions of men lay no small claim to the legend of treachery among women: "Women, like princes," said Lord Lyttelton in England, "find few real friends." "To speak the truth, I never yet knew a tolerable woman to be fond of her own sex," offered Jonathan Swift. "A woman depends upon her body far more than she realizes," wrote French novelist André Maurois. "She will always give first place to the man she loves physically, and if he insists, will renounce the most perfect friendship for him." "However bad the things a man may think about women," Sebastien Chamfort slyly observed in the eighteenth century, "there is no woman who does not think worse of them than he." A twenty-eight-year-old male survey respondent adds his comments:

"I believe that women are capable of authentic friendships but, truthfully, I don't see much of it around. It may be that they're victims of a prejudiced society—friendship is a luxury which the powerless cannot afford. When you cannot get what you want because of male domination, you learn to be underhanded; you discard people when they are no longer useful. I think this is what's happened to women. Whether it is winning a man, a position in a professional school or on the job market, the pickings have been slim and the competition very rough. That doesn't make for closeness. No, I'd say women do not have close relationships with other women. Female solidarity, as far as I can tell, is a lie perpetuated by the women's movement. All they seem to do is reinforce each other in their victim roles. That's not what friendship is about."

Even the popular media deal with female friendship as a joke. Lucy and Ethel ("The Lucy Show"), Rhoda and Mary ("The Mary Tyler Moore Show"), Veronica and Betty ("Archie Comics"), Alice and Trixie ("The Honeymooners") are all relationships played for laughs and centered on men. They are farcical. In movies, women have been treated as second-class citizens—as hookers or tight-lipped virgins, as larger-than-life sex objects or goofy homemakers, always as vacuous supporting characters in the male drama. Serious friendships among women—as contrasted with fill-ins between romances—are a subject so rarely written about that it almost seems forbidden.

Are women wary of each other? Is the warmth of feeling that women are said to express toward men held in abeyance or transformed into hatred when directed at their sisters? Sisterhood may be powerful, but is it marred by mistrust and an ancient tradition of rivalry? Do women, entrapped by their roles, place little emphasis on friendship? All of the negative answers offered in the past are simple and clear-cut; they have a great surface appeal. But the odds and ends of "proof" on which they are based do not constitute scientific evidence; nearly all of us are prone to collect views which bolster our opinions, while walking blindly past those that contradict them. Going directly to the source—women themselves—in great numbers, leads to a more reliable answer, though surely not a simple one. As we shall see, some notions surrounding women and their friendships were confirmed; many were denied.

Looking Behind the Myths: Some Findings

"One problem in acquiring female friends," a thirty-one-year-old woman wrote, "is that for years women have been influenced to regard their own sex as secondary. Because of this, they often haven't the slightest notion of how to get close to one another on anything but a superficial level." A similar sentiment was echoed by several women:

To attach too much importance to friendships with women is adolescent.

Secretary, 24

It will be viewed as "latent" lesbianism.

Computer Programmer, 22

If you're single, other women regard a close female bond as evidence of not having made the grade in the competition for men.

Elementary Schoolteacher, 38

Interesting women choose the company of men; they do not seek out or open up to other women.

Attorney, 41

My need to confide in another woman is often hampered by a competitive need to prove that my marriage is happier than hers.

Housewife, 39

It is evident that some women devalue their affectional ties with their peers. In contrast to the popular myth, however, they are in a minority. More often, women report a great deal of intimacy and self-revelation with each other. Fifty-three percent stated that they had a close friend with whom they felt free to discuss intimate feelings. This might include feelings of competition with other women for male attention, sexual issues and problems in love relationships. As one woman stated:

"I have a great need to keep the feeling atmosphere clear with my female friends. We are seldom content to lay a problem aside, or to gloss over difficulties in our lives or between ourselves. My experience has been mostly positive; I have not been hurt by my honesty. Quite to the contrary, being expressive about loneliness, anxiety or my joys has made it easier for friends to relate to me."

Although disloyalty and betrayal were burning issues that

touched the lives of women, their experiences were more often demonstrative of support and sympathy; they counted on one another physically and psychically. When they are ill, depressed or in need of a favor, in the majority of instances, it is another woman to whom they turn. A thirty-seven-year-old department-store saleswoman spoke proudly of feminine allegiance:

"Last year my father died. For months I was besieged with despair. He and my mother were married thirty-nine years—up until the day he died they held hands and wrote love letters to each other. The men in my life—my husband, some of our friends —really didn't appreciate how I felt about the loss. They were uncomfortable with my grief. It was my women friends who came through. They are the ones who braved my unkempt house where I sat sobbing, and offered me a sympathetic shoulder to cry on."

And this from a fifty-four-year-old bank teller: "I had just ended a painful extramarital affair. It was a cold, damp winter morning and I called my friend Sarah and invited her for lunch. She felt my distress and received my confession. Even though not an intimate friend, she responded to my emptiness. She asked me to spend the rest of the day with her. I was touched. We talked. I told her of my marital difficulties; she confided in me. We felt very close."

A waitress, forty-eight, added her vote of confidence: "I don't know if women are psychologically stronger than men or what, but my basic feeling is that if I had to do battle for something involving real survival, I would want another woman fighting with me. In a crisis, women seem to be gutsier than men. . . . I know of a woman who was raped. When she needed people to go to court for her she couldn't persuade any of the men in her life to offer support. It was her female friends who came through. This woman no longer has anything to do with those men. When I met her and she recounted this horror story she said, 'I may not be a feminist, but I know loyalty when I see it and I am forever grateful to my sisters.' "

The fact is, a lot more women are trustful of one another than is typically supposed. Even of those who did not have a close friend with whom to discuss personal matters, the great majority —over eighty percent—placed at least some value on friendship. It was a rare woman so totally obsessed with the role of home-maker and mother or so enmeshed in her career that she completely ignored friendship needs. Thus, although the desire for friendship may be unsatisfied in nearly half of our female respond-ents, they may be more open to the experience than the testimony of fiction leads us to believe. Further, women see each other and themselves in a much less stereotyped manner than would be pre-dicted. Asked to list traits they felt were desirably feminine, sixty-eight percent consistently crossed sex-role lines. They in-cluded typically "female" characteristics in their responses— tender, expressive, sensitive, emotional and giving. But they named "male" qualities as well—assertive, independent, active, ambitious and tough. As a thirty-six-year-old teacher wrote:

"Women were always reserved for my everyday survival. They were the ones I turned to for a favor—to take care of my apart-ment when I was away, or to drive cross-town and sit up all night with me in a crisis. Men were for my intellectual and emotional stimulation; they were for 'real life'; women were for getting through the day. What bound me to my girlfriends was our problems. But the price of these friendships was that they were short-lived. When you became strong you became unacceptable, and the friendship fell apart. My male friends were the ones I'd turn to for ideas; they were the ones I really respected. Women were for using. . . . I don't know when it happened, when I gave up my stereotypes about men and women. All I know is I now feel different—different about myself and about my friends. I am now enjoying more satisfying, more complete friendships with other women."

Although women overwhelmingly favored other women as close friends and confidantes, some reported a preference for men in this role. In these instances, occupational doubts and love relationships are primary topics of conversation; rarely are the details of sexuality discussed. Those women who did not have a close friend of either sex with whom to share the personal experiences of their daily lives expressed significant feelings of loneliness and depression three times more often than their friendship-involved counterparts. Notable in this regard was a distinct trend encompassing four out of five lonely women: Feelings of friendless isolation were not due to shyness, as might be expected, nor did interviews reveal other personal barriers to friendship—distrust of people, unpleasant characteristics or a lack of social feeling. The key was circumstance; the great majority of these women were housewives.

For women, particularly as their numbers increase in the job market, the work place is not only an important source of money and accomplishment, it is a clearinghouse of friendship and camaraderie. From factory worker to executive, women spoke of co-workers—friends on the job—as a source of great pleasure. When asked about the rewards of work, women offer the standard reason—for the money, to be sure—but it is not *just* for the money. The need to be with people, make social contacts and possibly build friendships was mentioned as often as financial benefits. One woman, recently returned to the work force after five years as a homemaker, explains:

"My old friendships have been dissolved through either relocation or divorce and the changes that brings. Some have just fizzled out, and we have gone our separate ways. Living in a neighborhood where people pretty much keep to themselves, I felt quite isolated and unhappy. The thought of moving even occurred to me—maybe to a co-op or to a friendlier community or something—but my husband wouldn't hear of it. I held out as mother and homemaker for a while, but when being alone all day started to feel like jail, I made up my mind to find a babysitter and return to nursing. What I was looking for was social interaction; developing a new set of friends was my main objective. As a matter of fact, I quit my first job even though it had obvious benefits—good salary, convenience, pleasant conditions—and took a lower-paying position with a longer commute in a bustling, active teaching hospital. I did it simply for the increased opportunity to meet people."

Joining the occupational force is one way of increasing one's social network. Including both single and married persons in a friendship circle is another. In this regard it might be expected that women would not abandon each other because of different marital status. Unfortunately, this is not the case. When women were questioned about their friends, very few, only two out of ten, had any friends whose marital status differed from their own.

Speaking of these experiences, single women felt carelessly abandoned. Nursing feelings of hurt and rejection, they complained that their married friends were "swallowed up" by their husbands. Many married women confirmed this. "I find myself under a great deal of pressure from my husband," wrote one woman. "I make an appointment with a girlfriend for an evening and he demands that I spend the evening with him. 'Who's more important?' is how he puts it. I try to explain importance has nothing to do with it, but to no avail."

Of course, in some cases it is the single woman who rejects the now-married friend. Marjorie is twenty-four, fresh out of Vassar with a master's degree in literature. She is working for a major publisher in Manhattan. Hers is the life of chic discos and flamboyant summer weekends on the east end of Long Island. While in high school, she was part of a large group of girls; in college, she found less need for a crowd and formed a close relationship with one girl, Rachel.

"Rachel and I hit it off instantly. We roomed together, went out dancing, visited museums, made music, did everything together. When college ended, Rachel married a guy from back home who was now a corporate attorney. She bought the whole conventional number—moved to the suburbs, joined a bunch of ladies' groups and settled down with her station wagon and two-car garage. I couldn't see it at all. I was bridesmaid at her wedding, but afterward we just drifted apart. We went through the motions of getting together once in a while, for obligatory lunch dates, but frankly, I wasn't interested; it's just that I have difficulty breaking off the relationship with a determined goodbye."

And what of those rare instances when a friendship between a single woman and a married woman endures? The answers came through unanimously: The friends most apt to last are those with whom we have shared crucial times and who change as we change; marital status is critical only if values and "styles" become too discordant.

Disruptions

The struggle for women to accept each other as friends has not been easy, nor is it complete. Many women are seeking serious relationships with one another based on mutual respect, a healthy exchange of ideas and the simple enjoyment of each other's company. Others still form relationships with each other for reasons that are less than noble: so they can have a sympathetic shoulder to lean on when a man is unavailable, or a willing listener to brag to when romance and career are going well, or simply to fill empty time, those occasions when there is nothing better to do.

When women were asked about the elements that interfered with friendship, the related factors of competition and betrayal—accusations that have plagued them for ages—were reported more often than any other common source of conflict (in order of frequency): lack of time for friendship; different interests; conflicting values; low self-disclosure. As numerous sociologists of both sexes have pointed out, women are as capable of showing scorn for each other as other "marginal," oppressed peoples—blacks, Jews and Hispanics, to name a few. To a woman living on the periphery of a male society and longing to be accepted by the dominant group, the safest recipients of her rage are others of her sex.

Basically, it came down to the old guidelines. If women want to keep peace in their friendships: Don't make a pass at a friend's man; don't undermine her job opportunities; and don't betray her confidence. In addition to these mainstays of competition and betrayal, the act of subordinating friendship to male preference is considered by many women, especially those who are single, to be highly damaging.

"You may have been seeing or talking with her on the phone almost daily; you've grown used to sharing the problems and joys of your life. Then, suddenly she pulls a disappearing act. She's met a man and automatically she drops you. When you call, she is preoccupied, distant. Sometimes she is evasive—probably feeling guilty about the sharp contrast in your relationship. You soothe yourself as best you can and tell yourself to forget it— 'that's how it is.' A few months go by and she calls—usually in the middle of the night—in crisis. The romance crumbled, it crashed; 'life isn't worth living, I can't go on,' she sobs. The lines are tired, worn out. Admittedly, I've uttered them in desperation myself a few times. . . . She expects to pick up the friendship where it was. So what do you do? You resume, you carry on— or at least you pretend to."

Perhaps it is insufficient self-love that accounts for women meekly deferring their friendships to the needs and wishes of men. Conditioning by a biased society that views women as inferior certainly doesn't bolster self-esteem. In any case, getting married offers little immunity; the betrayal does not necessarily dissolve, it merely takes a different form. In one instance, a married woman's lifelong friendship was destroyed when her jealous husband made a play for the friend. Although the friend was clearly innocent and her husband guilty, he was pardoned and she never forgiven.

When women spoke of their organizational memberships, the tenuity of the friendship grasp was once again demonstrated to be under the male influence: Most women readily admit that in addition to rendering a social service—in such groups as League of Women Voters, American Cancer Society, March of Dimes and the like—they are seeking friendship ties. Yet, in many instances where a close friendship may have developed, it was allowed to wane because the men in their lives—their husbands—were not compatible.

Those women who have swallowed whole the societal defamation of their sisters have come to hate their femaleness. The common but futile attempts to restore self-esteem by a strong identification with the dominant group (men) and a putdown of one's own group is another obvious detraction from friendship. Instead of admiring another woman for her occupational success, for example, the self-hater is likely to be hostile. This sometimes occurs to the woman who breaks sex-role barriers and climbs to a high-level professional position; instead of being warmly received, she is ostracized and penalized. It is one of the ironies of our time that women of accomplishment—pioneers who need supportive friendship—experience a good deal of rejection from other women. A thirty-seven-year-old attorney's experience:

"I forget who it was, but some French writer in the seventeenth century said something like, 'There is something not entirely displeasing in the misfortune of our close friends.' I can't say my experience contradicts this. I find it difficult to find friends who will delight in my happiness instead of resenting it. More than once I have found myself the unexpected target of another woman's wrath concerning my success. One woman went so far as to claim that 'I had no right taking a man's job!' I really don't know how to react when this occurs. It is not that I brag about my work or draw attention to my accomplishments; I don't. As a matter of fact, for a while I fell into a pattern of placating other women by deprecating myself. That was stupid and I no longer do it. Now I only choose other women as companions and friends who are my professional equals. I see this as unfortunate and a form of elitism, but there is just too much resentment any other way."

Contempt for self and kind is one basis for resentment toward another's accomplishment, but even more fundamental is our attitude toward winning and losing. All of us, men and women alike, have been bred to compete with one another and taught that winning makes you more worthwhile and losing, well, losing is for losers. Those women who believe this bring to their interactions a pressure that wards off closeness and intimacy. Friendship is bound to recoil from constant weighing and measuring, from the rationalizing of self-worth: She's better looking than I am but I'm brighter; she has a higher-paying job, mine is more prestigious; her marriage is stable and boring, my marriage is rocky but exciting.

Women spoke of competition and rivalry with mixed feelings. Some relished it, some were threatened by it, some few felt severely damaged by it, most could accept it up to a point. One thing was certain: Whether it is in soft focus or sharply defined, competition and rivalry were elements in practically every close female relationship; and in those instances where they were not a deterrent to friendship, the issue was out in the open. That is, when women admitted and spoke to each other about their feelings, the friendship prognosis improved. The act of denial poisoned the relationship as much as or more than competition itself.

Undeniably, women have been taught to compete with each other for men and, in more recent years, for jobs—even at the cost of friendship. However, feminine self-hate and the willingness to sacrifice a friendship to "get a man" or "land a job" has been grossly exaggerated by moviemakers—most of whom, it should be emphasized, are men. All of this notwithstanding, it is useless to pretend that betrayal and rivalry are not at issue, that they are manmade myths. Sisterhood is powerful, but so is the need to win; one-upmanship is built into the fabric of American society. Yet, many women have found a solution: They can talk about their problems and experiences. More often than not, the discovery of their common fate produces feelings of relief and a sense of solidarity.

What Do Women Want?

"For almost nineteen years, I have had a friendship, by turns ardent and fragile, with a woman whose imagination stimulates mine, whose emotions and spirit I prize. Each of us appears, sometimes dramatically, sometimes comically, in the other's dreams. She and I agree that we are of one soul." Thus wrote a forty-eight-year-old woman about a treasured person in her life. What is involved in such an enduring, solid relationship? If the dynamics of betrayal and competition keep women apart, what combination of ingredients draws them closer? Freud, toward the end of his life, bewailed the fact that even after years of investigation, he had never succeeded in finding out "what women want." If women are confusing, variable, unable or unwilling to express their wants, as Freud's statement suggests, this does not hold true for their feelings about friendship. There, most women have very definite standards.

Above all, women want a framework of openness and honesty in their friendships. The factor of emotional openness was mentioned as essential to closeness by virtually every woman. This isn't particularly surprising. All of us have hundreds of associations in which there is a mutual unspoken proscription against saying anything to irritate the other for fear of causing dislike. Consequently, the rule for maintaining many of our looser ties is deception; subtle lying becomes an art form in these relationships. In close friendships there is a hunger for the truth; a high premium is put on emotional integrity. "It is reassuring," one woman stated, "not to have to spend time guessing how the other person really feels, what she is really thinking."

As for the turbulence sometimes created by negative disclosures, this was an unresolved issue in the minds of many. Although it was generally opined that "really strong relationships would survive confrontations of this sort," countless women had stories of friendships fractured due to an overdose of openness. Feeling wounded, some women spoke of retreating into superficiality, but after a period of repair, most felt driven once again to approximate the ideal. "Any hint of insincerity," one woman explained, "puts me off!" With hardly an exception, ingratiates—people who say nice things that they don't really mean in order to secure personal gain or approval—were avoided for close friendship.

In addition to emotional openness, the importance of caring in cementing strong friendships was highlighted by the replies of over seven hundred women, three-quarters of the sample. Caring is an abstract idea that is difficult to define, but after speaking to many women it became evident that it is not just a matter of blind acceptance or unconditional love. Caring is understanding; it is a willingness to identify with the woes and joys of others, to put ourselves in their place, to have it really matter to us how they are faring. Emotional openness and caring exist in a delicate balance. It is in a climate of caring that women share intimacies, and it is the understanding of these personal disclosures that encourages a caring response.

Diane, a forty-four-year-old artist who teaches in Seattle, Washington, and who counts among her friends the raccoons that live in the woods near her home, had particularly strong feelings about the caring dimension:

"Caring doesn't mean rushing into action at every crisis and 'making it all better!' When a child falls and hurts herself, the mother who 'cares' too much glosses over the pain by mouthing words that are empty and unrealistic: 'There now, don't cry, that doesn't hurt.' What the child wants, though, is for her mother to understand how she really feels: 'There now, of course it hurts, no wonder you are crying. Soon it will mend and you will feel better.'

"For me, caring in an adult relationship is the same thing. If the quality of my work is disappointing, for example, I don't want someone to simply rationalize for me or entertain me into a frozen smile; someone who cares doesn't deny my feelings. I want instead someone who will listen carefully and try to understand. My close friends do that; they lend a sympathetic ear and offer constructive, honest advice when they have it—and when they sense I'm ready for it."

And finally, there is mental stimulation. For most women, it is not necessary to have identical interests or to be involved in the same activities in order to be friends. Rather than mutual endeavor, it is the nature of the reciprocal exchange that is crucial to the female friendship bond. In the best of female friendships different interests, activity preferences, habits, thoughts, feelings and idiosyncrasies are a basis for learning and self-extension. When these differences are not too sharp and they are perceived as desirable, there is joy and exhilaration in the exchange.

Particularly over the past two decades, the level of emotional/intellectual aspiration among women has risen dramatically. No longer content to be on the sidelines, women are seeking friends who challenge them and who will enhance their growth. "Friendship requires two alive, vital, growing individuals," said a nursery-school director. "I don't want a friend to be another self, at least not in the sense of being an echo." A young freelance writer expressed a similar thought: "Continued friendship is impossible unless there is intellectual rapport. I look for an exchange of ideas and the challenge of someone who can help me see things from a different perspective." Another woman, separated from a friend for several years, discussed their meeting:

"After a while, the conversation began to sink; the old stories had been rehashed and there was nothing to talk about. It dawned on me that our connection was broken; she did not understand what I was talking about and I saw her as stagnant. Simply, my experience while we were apart had taken me beyond the friendship. It was sad; there was a sense of loss, but I had outgrown her. I feel shrewish saying it, but she was boring."

Making friends may be a frustrating matter for all of us, but keeping friends is surely the more difficult and complex issue. There are numerous factors that can contribute to close friendships—similarity in interests, responsiveness in a crisis, loyalty and the mysterious alchemy that defies definition—but for women it is openness, caring and mental stimulation which rank highest. These are the ingredients women consider to be essential for developing a casual friendship into a more devoted and permanent bond.

It is important for women to understand these factors and to appreciate what it means to have and to be a true friend. Lack of clarity can lead to the acceptance of substitutes; acquaintanceship that simulates friendship may be taken for the real thing. Playing tennis with a woman once a week, for example, seeing her at work daily, living next door to her or belonging to the same organization doesn't necessarily qualify for close friendship. When the activity ends, when the circumstance changes, the "friendship" is likely to be discarded unless the "essentials" are present to transcend the change. Of course, few people are likely to meet these criteria to perfection. And standards ought not be set so high that they inevitably lead to disappointment. Henry Adams was realistic about the challenge: "One friend in a lifetime is much; two are many; three are hardly possible," he wrote.

The Friendship Cycle: An Odyssey

Great masses of data have been accumulated about specific features of adult life. There are statistics on marriage and divorce, health and illness, life expectancy, occupation, sexuality and income. There are studies of such stressful events as retirement, the "empty nest" syndrome and death in the family. We have, in short, extensive information on adulthood. There is, however, one glaring omission—the developmental principles of friendship remain an enigma; the overall shape of friendship through various stages of life is uncharted. Although opinions abound, research in this area is practically nonexistent. By tracing the course of friendship among our female respondents, a definable form began to evolve; the cycles of their friendship odyssey emerged.

"When I was eight, I had lots of girlfriends. I lived in an apartment house loaded with other kids. As soon as I came home from school, I ran to my group of friends; we were inseparable. For four years we adored each other and provided support for one another. When someone had a falling out with her parents, we always took her side; we echoed each other's opinions about particular teachers; we helped each other with homework and made sure no one was left out of activities. We were really quite sensitive and concerned with each other. At fourteen I shifted gears. I became more interested in being admired by the boys than in friendship. I left all my friends by the wayside. Jane was the only one from that group I kept up with; she was my closest friend when I was younger, and throughout my teens she was the only one I really felt attached to. Other girls became competitors. If they were more attractive than I, I copied their look, their style. Those who were less attractive became nonthreatening companions; at least they wouldn't steal the boys. But, except for Jane, I never related to any of them as people. They were pawns in the dating game; uninteresting pawns at that. All of us, myself included, were very unidimensional—striving for one thing: to prove our worth by the status of the boy we dated. Even then, at the tender age of sixteen, we were heavily invested in male achievement. To go out with a football player, the class president, Mr. Popularity, that was success.

"After I finished high school, I went through another transition. I continued to rate myself by the male in my life, but I missed the pleasures of friendship. My romantic connections weren't enough; I sought camaraderie again—among the boys. They were still the interesting ones: Men had jobs and made money. Women were responsible for housekeeping. Men got to be doctors, engineers and lawyers; women became nurses, elementary schoolteachers and secretaries. It was my Dad who went to football games and boxing matches. My mother got to mop the floor and cook the meals. When my father's friends came over to the house, they drank, horsed around, talked about sports and seemed to have serious, important business together. The women served. Men, it seemed, talked about ideas, important things. They were dynamic, anxious to better themselves. Women seemed passive, too content, boring. Small wonder I wanted to be 'one of the guys.' But the boys had different ideas—most of them emanating from the crotch! I wanted a close, nonsexual relationship, but it never worked out that way. Relationships that started out to be stimulating and friendly had a way of coming to a crisis: 'Either we have sex or we part. I don't need a brother-sister relationship,' I was told on more than one occasion. You know, it wasn't until a few years later that I realized I was being told, 'You are valued as a body, as a sexual receptacle, not as a person.' Interesting—I viewed other women as objects; men viewed me the same way. Where did that leave me?

"Married—that's where it left me. I was married in my early twenties, and four years and two children later we moved cross-country to California. The women on the block became my 'friends.' These were easy, smiling relationships; they were all anxious to make friends and, as a newcomer, I was invited to endless lunches, mid-afternoon shopping sprees, etc. Some of the women from the neighborhood had other women friends that I met and my associations with women grew into quite a network. Most of my free time was spent sitting over coffee with several other women trading gossip and watching the kids. We all had small children and were married to men heavily involved in careers. We were like a band of single parents surviving together. Sometimes conversation even became a physical challenge, words uttered between screams and shoving cookies into small, insatiable mouths. Then there were the occasional parties—I met two kinds of women at the parties, the edgy rivals and the housewives. The housewives huddled together and spoke of washing machine overflows, burnt toast, the time Johnny fell down and cut his head open. The rivals, dressed to the hilt, circled each other in careful appraisal, checking the curve of a figure, the low-cut dress, the hair style. While the toilet-training crowd was beginning to bore me to distraction, my tolerance for my venomous sisters, gazing at themselves in full-length mirrors, was also on the low side.

"I personally enjoyed being a woman, but my bias against women was increasing. One incident in particular was dramatic. On a visit back to New York, I stopped in to see my old friend Jane. As kids we were able to talk forever. Now, after an exchange of amenities, I was shocked to discover I could hardly fill thirty seconds of conversation with her. There were dirty diapers all over the place, dishes in the sink, chaos all around. Jane looked distressingly unkempt, worn out, harassed. Maybe my disappointment was the product of raised expectations—I was hoping Jane would be an oasis, a breath of fresh air among beaten or rivalrous women—but she was trapped also. She, too, was engrossed in her children's sleeping habits, their bowel movements, her husband's career. When we had been friends I was interested in *her*; now the *her* had disappeared. We sat around the table sipping the familiar cup of coffee and pretended we still had a connection. But it was over. The externals of our lives were not terribly dissimilar, but our souls had grown miles apart. The friendship was a memory to me now. Partly, I felt sad and lonely. Was this going to be my plight? Was I going to resign myself to being somebody's mother, somebody's wife? Will my ideas and dreams vanish as I associate with women who have suppressed their individuality? Will my spirit ebb? On my return to California I was resolved to reenter the market for women friends. This time I was going to make a herculean effort to find women who were also groping to discover themselves.

"That first week back in town, two years ago now, I joined a women's group. This proved to be an enormous step toward getting to know myself and other women from a totally different perspective. The women in the group are stimulating, alive. They are a challenge to my antiwomen bias. Ironically, these women aren't extraordinary. They may well be the same women I rejected as friends all these years. I look at my own womanhood differently now; I am more sympathetic to my own struggle in a man's world. Consequently, I relate to other women's lives more sympathetically. When I look more closely at those parties I so dreaded, for example, I have a different view of things. The women clustered in the 'recipe swapping' corner were frequently squeezed out of the men's conversations and looked to each other for support. Those conversations among women, as meager as they may have seemed to me, were often their only acknowledgment as human beings of worth—they shared a common struggle. Other women, those I characterized as rivalrous, simply chose a different way to say, 'I want recognition also.' I can understand that, it no longer seems contemptuous. Actually, it's quite human. These days I work on my relationships with other women. I invest in them. And you know what—they ripen. I have a few good, close friends. I am quite pleased with that."

Friendship among women is a drama which unfolds in four acts: Act One, the preadolescent girl chooses a girlfriend who resembles her and who, like herself, feels insignificant and needs a faithful confidante; Act Two, during the adolescent phase, boys enter the picture and friendship loyalties are divided by romantic conflict; Act Three, the young woman marries or forms a close romantic tie and views women as supplements to her life; Act Four, after several years of indifference, becoming friends with another woman begins to assume a renewed importance.

Of course, the friendship pattern of each individual has its own special character and follows its own complex path; all conclusions about human beings are likely to have notable exceptions. Nonetheless, some general observations on the sequence of events do apply.

Preadolescence. The majority of women (seventy-nine percent) report having had one special friend. In practically every instance (ninety-eight percent of the time), the early relationship was with someone of the same sex.

Of the twenty-one percent not having a best friend at this age, more than half describe themselves as shy. Presumably they, too, would have liked a close ally but were inhibited by self-consciousness. To a preadolescent, even more than friendship in general, a best friend of her own age and sex—one to whom she can passionately attach herself—is held dear. Women spoke of this "first friend" in especially tender terms: "We loved each other"; "we just couldn't imagine anything or anyone coming between us"; "we were always together and thinking of each other"; "Janice and I were like sisters." The events and contexts of childhood—embracing one another with tenderness, walking arm in arm, whispering confidences to one another, sleeping at each other's houses—are cherished memories to many women.

Adolescence. This is a turbulent time when there is a great deal to think about and to talk about—girls once again have a constant companion. This was true eighty-one percent of the time (in approximately one out of three instances, this is the same friend from younger days). The two friends become emotionally dependent on each other, talk on the phone for hours, share homework assignments and, most importantly, go out looking for boys together; they become cruising partners.

Women spoke of their adolescent cruising partner/best friend relationships as less idyllic than earlier friendships. Added to the usual adolescent guardedness and private turmoil—independent-dependent struggles, identity crises, and the like—was competition for the attention of boys. In an effort to avoid conflict while capitalizing on the benefits of companionship, the friendship pairings most sought were of different types—not better or worse looking—but complementary. At this sensitive age, nothing works as quickly to end a friendship as attracting or being attracted by the same man.

While women most often characterized their preteen friendships as "inseparable," a different code operated for the teen years, particularly the late teens. An unspoken provision often existed during these years that if one of them should get serious about a man, it was time for the other to find a new "best" friend. Women commonly describe these partings as troubled; bitterness and envy lingered in the unattached, guilt in the newly coupled. Sometimes the provisional nature of the friendship was mutually understood—"we both know that developing a romantic relationship is a prime objective"—and the parting was more amicable.

Marriage, Early Years. The American dream of husband and family is sought by many women in their twenties. In fact, three-quarters of married women and more than half of those unmarried view this decade as being least productive of close friendships. Consistently enough, as a group, women in this age range expressed a lower desire for female companionship than did women at other ages. Speaking of these years, women explained that shouldering the combined weight of family and career allowed precious little time to the pursuit of friendship. Other women were regarded less as friends and more as diversions when a husband or lover was unavailable. For single women, the indifference to female camaraderie was most evident when previous plans made with a woman were canceled to go out with a man. As an extension of the adolescent code, stranded "friends" were expected to understand.

Once married, a woman's same-sex friends are likely to be a neighbor, the wife of one of her husband's business associates, the mother of her child's playmate, or a friend from the past. With the long-standing friend, the former closeness is dormant; the relationship has been transformed from intimate to companionable. With the others—neighbors, business connections and fellow mothers—the tenuous character of the relationship becomes apparent when there is a move to another locality. Promises may be exchanged to keep in touch, but once separation occurs and after a flurry of letters, they eventually forget each other.

Transitional Thirties. Friendship with other women comes full circle; in their early thirties the attitude of wasting time with other women slowly dissolves and is replaced by a realization that women are interesting human beings. This is a time when the values of sisterhood and relating are renewed; the intimacy of old friendships is often restored and new friendships are pursued enthusiastically. During this period the greatest proportionate number of women considered friendship at least moderately important in their lives. Not unexpectedly, this was proportionately the period most productive of close adult friendships; the number of women actually having close friendships—relationships reminiscent in feeling tone of preteen years, but on a more mature level —rises dramatically during the thirties and holds steady through the fifties.

So it is with the female friendship drama: The performance may falter at times but, as the final act develops, there is for most women movement toward contact. A growing number of women share an awareness and concern for each other's situational and psychological condition. This may be partially due to the cultural change in recent years which encourages women to develop their own standards instead of embracing the masculine code. Rather than rejecting femaleness—"being a man's woman"— women are discovering opportunities for spiritual and emotional growth with each other. "They are," in one woman's words, "making themselves available to other women personally and professionally."

Men and Friendship:
Noble Companions or Companionable Competitors?

Brotherhood Idealized

WHILE FRIENDSHIPS BETWEEN WOMEN have been debased in myth, song and story, the friendships of men have been sung and celebrated throughout the ages. Whether the seed of male camaraderie is germinated through confronting crises at work, war, on the political front or the athletic field, it is believed to be flourishing. Forged through shared experiences, male friendship is depicted in movies, novels and dramas as the ultimate in commitment and acceptance. Paul Newman and Robert Redford as Butch Cassidy and the Sundance Kid portray the ideal: two men of equal stature linked together against the world.

From childhood the young boy is drawn to other males. He learns to copy his father's behavior—he observes his style of dress, the way he talks, swears, throws a baseball and drinks his beer—and comes to value his membership in the male world. He looks forward to the promise of comradeship among men: A man will do anything for his buddy. He'll bail him out of a jam at great risk to life and limb. He'll lend him money to start a business, get out of debt or get drunk. He'll welcome a buddy to his home when he is no longer welcome in his own. He'll come out in the middle of the night to stand by his side in a crisis. He'll listen, respond, offer advice and inspiration. He's a buddy, he can be counted on.

Male Friendship. It is ritualized as strong and characterized in glowing terms: devotion, honesty, trust, selflessness; a loyalty held above life. The legends are plentiful and rich with epic tales of friendships to the death, unity overshadowing the ties of blood relatives: David and Jonathan, Damon and Pythias are memorialized by virtue of their friendship. Each was prepared to sacrifice life itself for his friend. Jonathan jeopardized his right to the throne and braved the murderous wrath of his father, King Saul, by refusing to betray David. Damon resolved to stand execution in his friend's place and was moments away from death when Pythias, who might have fled and saved himself, returned to perish.

It is a fine tradition. A young Butch Cassidy can look forward to teaming up with some future Sundance Kid; together they will defy adversity, they will stand by each other to the bitter end. This is the ideal. But how much of this accepted representation of male friendship materializes, and how much is Hollywood myth? The fact is that male friendships rarely live up to the ideal. Although men do prefer the company of other men—they prefer men to drink with, play games with and work with—an air of wariness pervades their contact. As much as he might yearn for closer friends, a man soon realizes that business and friendship don't mix; that you can't trust anyone with your wife or girlfriend (not even your best friend); that other men are potential rivals.

In short, my survey sharply contradicts the legend. Adolescence, a time that most males remember as rich with friendship, is the last time many men recall having an intense same-sex relationship. Memories of these early attachments run deep, and many men were able to summon images of these long-past events with such clarity it was as if they occurred yesterday. Yet, despite their hunger for the "good old days," the majority see other men as allies or enemies, but only a minority really have friends. In our achievement-oriented society, men are encouraged to put all their energy into getting ahead. Closeness with other human beings, particularly other men—adversaries to be conquered or avoided —is regarded as an unaffordable luxury. Rather than living in a land of plentiful friendship, most men are lonely, a feeling they often soothe philosophically: "It's every man for himself," they remind themselves.

Male Friendships: Reality

Upon being interviewed about their comrades, men frequently spoke of distrust and only occasionally of loyalty. Having learned caution, they expected neither sympathy nor devotion from their brothers. On the contrary, their experiences are filled with incidents of rivalry and betrayal. Eighty-four percent dare not disclose themselves fully to other men. Relying heavily on activity —drinking, playing or watching sports, for instance—to connect with other males, most shy away from intimacy. Particularly does this hold true in matters sexual. Only eight out of a hundred acknowledge having had a frank sexual discussion with a buddy. Even more sensitive than sexuality is a man's ambitions. In-depth interviews reveal that becoming competent and well respected in an occupation weighs heavily on the male soul. Getting ahead or staying on top was often in the forefront of conversation. The emphasis was on doing, making, having. Whatever occupational arena—from automobile mechanic to physician—the wish to establish his place and accomplish his goals was dominant. Wives, children and friendship were, with a few exceptions, far back in the field.

Quite simply, men anticipated and were frightened by the harsh judgment of their fellows. It was critically important to be seen by other men as confident, successful and sexually assured. Weaknesses were not about to be disclosed for fear of attack. "If I tell another man I'm not confident in my abilities on the job, he might try for it," one man explained. Another corresponded: "If I tell a friend my wife isn't satisfied with our sex, I would be scared to death that my buddy would say, 'Uhm, maybe I ought to go over there and lend him a hand.'" Beyond betrayal, my respondents feared appearing unmanly. Being scared, unsure or emotional was deemed a violation of the masculine cult of toughness and independence. This was highlighted when respondents were asked to list traits they felt were desirably masculine. They answered, almost as with one voice: aggressive, independent, unemotional, dominant, competitive, logical, blunt, tough. Indeed, they conduct their friendships as if they have to be constantly poised to defy insinuations that they do not measure up to the masculine standard.

If a man is given a choice of confidants with whom to discuss feelings, doubts and fears, he is twice as likely to prefer a woman to another man. About half the men sampled chose solitude; they confide in no one. Those taking this "strong and silent" trip more often report feelings of moderate loneliness and depression (seventy-three percent as compared to twenty-eight percent of other male respondents). Presumably blocked by manly pride, these men refuse to heed the cries of their psyche and will not reach out for support. Apparently, despite the pain and loneliness of their posture, they will not challenge the male code and turn honestly to one another for help. Some of these men expressed the notion that if they burdened another man with their problems, they would be obligated. Being open was viewed as a debt that required repayment. Rather than be asked for help at some later date, they practiced self-sufficiency to an extreme. Occasionally, some men chose strangers—men or women with whom they did not have to compete or whom they did not see socially—to unburden themselves. As one man, a bartender, put it:

"There are many men who come in very occasionally who are looking to unload. When I'm busy I try to get them started in a conversation with another guy, which usually isn't very difficult. If I have time, I feel him out myself and see what's on his mind. Men whose names I don't even know have confessed their affairs to me, talked about their business problems, debts, girlfriends, bosses, you name it. They've poured their hearts out and I might not see them again for weeks or months."

Almost three out of four men reported wide social networks containing amicable "friendly" relationships with other men. This might include a coworker, a neighbor, a golf partner, patrons of a local tavern. But these are more appropriately termed acquaintances. When the use of the term friend is tightened—someone you feel close to, see often, can count on when you need him—four out of five men declared themselves to be friendless. Only one in five had an intimate male friend of the kind that they recall fondly from their youth—someone they could turn to, a companion who enriches their life. In interviews, some of these friendless men did not see the lack of a male intimate as unusual; their posture was cool, matter of fact, unemotional. They presented themselves as above it all, not in need. One man, aged fifty-four, the manager of a large travel agency, expressed particularly strong sentiments:

"The average American guy is a fellow who, when he stands up to offer his friend a hand, has his other hand clenched—just in case. I don't blame him a bit. The guy with the outstretched hand and no clout in reserve is a fool. I believe with Durocher that nice guys finish last. You might get your turn, but by then everybody will be out to lunch. . . . Sure, sure I have pals. These are guys I can count on in a clinch. But they're *not* friends. I can't afford friends. Too many times I have had to cut somebody's balls off in order to save mine. I can't do that if people are too close. You don't make money with friendships; you can't reach the moon, achieve your dream, run a business on friendships. A lot of people don't understand that. That's not how you stay on top. You hold your position by being a step ahead, by staying ahead. You need contacts who owe you. Those aren't friends; they'd drop you in a minute given the right circumstances. The people I am close to aren't friends, they are kin, family. My family—I can relax with them. I can trust them. You might say I have associates, guys who do for me because they need me to do for them, enemies whom I've hurt and who are looking to hurt me, and family who are loyal. I have no friends."

Another man, younger and less bitter, shared a similar disinterest in comradeship: "Friends are not terribly important to me. I have a lot of acquaintances but no real close friends. It's partly because I've moved a lot and also because I travel so much. But honestly, it's also largely due to not pursuing friendships. I'm happy to be by myself, reading or watching television when I'm not involved in work. There are guys at work I'm friendly with, but that's just convenience—we cover for each other when we're late or take a long lunch, that sort of thing. But it doesn't go further than that. We know little about each other nor is there any desire to know more. I guess the most social thing I do is play ball with some regulars. But even there, after we play, all we talk about is tennis. It never goes any further than that."

Although men such as the two quoted above claimed satisfaction with the status quo, it was clear as men talked about their relations with other men that most were in need of male support. They looked to each other with a deeper longing than mere companionship. What they wanted was to be understood and accepted, to fulfill the youthful promise of camaraderie. The point is, they didn't often receive it or, for that matter, trust it when they did. As several men expressed: Support is rarely given graciously without strings. Countless times men rationalized their anger, hurt and frustration regarding unrealized friendships through complaints that their peers were "fucked up," "too uptight," "depressive," "boring," "too withdrawn," "no fun to be with."

Men are caught in a bind. From both ends of the continuum they erect barriers to intimacy with their fellow men. The majority are not comfortable sharing their dark side—their anxieties and disappointments—for fear of being seen as weak or losers. Yet neither are they willing to rejoice openly in their successes for fear of being toppled by competitive jealousy. Afraid to be intimate, and lonely when they aren't, men only fleetingly progress beyond the externals, a limitation resulting in shallow relationships. There is, of course, no simple or single reason that can account for the state of male friendships. Each man is complex and the nature of his same-sex relations is the result of a combination of psychological and social forces. Yet, despite the complexity, male friendships, I found, were confounded—on a large scale—by three interrelated factors: overzealous rivalry, low self-disclosure and a fear of appearing unmanly. Below, a detailed look.

Top Dog/Bottom Dog

Of the many reasons why male friendship is so rare, competition—two men circling each other, each measuring who is the bigger, the faster, the stronger, the richer—occupies a high place on the list of obstacles. One man, a northeastern appliance repairman nearing thirty, described his experience:

"One way or another, men are always measuring. And everything counts. My handball matches are played as if my life depended on it. The essence of the game is not skill; it is crushing the other player, psychologically beating him down. Working on my car with another man at my side is the same thing. If I can't fix something, I'm not going to just say it. This guy's going to think I'm inferior. I'm going to cover up, make it seem like I know what I'm doing, that I need a part or something. In a conversation

I also feel the pressure. You strive to drive home a point. You make it logical, organized and persuasive. The game is, My Expertise Tops Yours, and victory is the main objective, with being authoritative an important tactic. Dominance and control, that's the thing. That's the way it is. He's checking you out and you're checking him out. Why should I leave myself open?"

A suburban dweller, thirty-eight, wrote: "It's like two dogs sniffing each other out. Is this guy ok? What does he do? How much does he make? What about his athletic ability? How does he deal with women? Can he help me? Is he looking for something from me? All these issues run through my head in an instant. Sure a friendship can develop, but only after we put these questions to the test—after we see who's on top and who's on bottom. It's like having a fight. As as kid I remember becoming friends with a guy after we had it out. It's a great release of tension, especially if we're evenly matched and nobody gets seriously hurt. It's like saying, 'Hey, you're ok and I'm ok. Both of us can take it. We've proved our courage, our manliness. Now we can relax. We can team up and sniff out other guys.' Having to prove yourself—passing through the rites of male friendship— seems to be almost as prevalent as when I was a kid. The major difference now is that men seem either avoidant of other men— buried in their success trips—or more civilized and subtle in the sniffing."

Roger Nichols, a midwestern real-estate agent, forty-three, has for the past few winters taken an ice-fishing vacation with several other men. This year Philip, a successful dentist, was the only other one of the group able to get away. Bonding was what Nichols hoped for; rivalry tempered slightly by an air of pseudocooperation was more his due.

"I expected a full complement this year and was pretty disappointed that the other guys couldn't make it. The trip had become a tradition—no shaving, very little washing, a lot of drinking and getting into the rough. It just wasn't the same without a crowd; it was a much different experience. Philip and I had been casual friends for a few years, but we never were really close—actually, I don't think I've felt particularly close to any man. So, in a way, although I was let down about the other guys not going—and I almost backed out myself, feeling uneasy going up with just one other guy—I decided to do it. The thought had occurred to me over the past year or two that I did not have any close friends. Maybe this would be a start.

"It didn't work out that way. We had a reasonably good time, the fish were really running, we got a lot of card playing in, but there was a definite feeling of competition between us. Every encounter became a contest which I felt I had to win or at least hold my own. The major area for the contest was who had the best catch each day. There was also a certain amount of rivalry over preparing the food and building the fire in the cabin—the survival tasks. I felt like a kid back in grade school; I, like most little boys, was taught that I must compete, that I must be aggressive. I must not be weak, not let on to feelings of weakness, tenderness or dependence, particularly to other men. My parents, relatives, my older brother, all taught me that my self-worth depended on my manliness, my willingness to 'fight like a man.' This lesson was reinforced everywhere—my teachers ('Oh, Roger, crying is for sissies'), the books I read, the movies I saw all presented an unquestionable definition of male identity.

"During the last weekend we were there, a woman who had been a patient of Phil's and who lived nearby stopped in. This was a very outgoing lady with a vibrant presence. The change in both of us was dramatic; the cabin filled with energy. It was as if she acted as a catalyst for us to relate. Early on she asked rather innocently, 'How're you guys getting along?' With her we were able to be a bit more open; a lot of hidden resentment surfaced. For the first time we acknowledged the tension, we admitted the lack of cooperation between us. She looked at us, puzzled. It must have seemed so petty to her. But it's not really so strange; after all, our behavior was not terribly different from that of most men with whom I'm familiar. Frankly, I don't know any men who are willing to give much energy or attention or emotion to each other—except maybe homosexuals. I mean, when was the last time you heard two straight men saying: 'I feel nervous talking to you like this' or, 'I really wonder how you feel about me'? Men are wary of the guy who talks like that—he's thought of as either a hopeless neurotic or a faggot."

Roger Nichols, a man describing himself as a product of his times—"a real man must be extremely independent, self-contained, emotionally invulnerable and nonexpressive of feelings"—has grown increasingly dissatisfied with his friendless, isolated existence. Outwardly he's the very model of a successful man, but beneath his protective armor he has begun to realize that his drive to win is costly. Even those he calls friends would be unable to say they really know him. They like him and think of him as a decent, "nice guy," but he knows that they don't see him as he is—driving, sometimes frightened, and a frequently lonely man. Asking his friends to try and define him was revealing: Without exception they wound up saying that he's pretty much unknown to them as a person. Roger used to rationalize his loneliness and isolation by telling himself he's basically a "private person; people aren't worth the effort." He no longer does this. Rather, he recognizes that he has not only limited his friendship relationships by his single-mindedness ("take away business and sports as topics of conversation and I may as well be mute"), but has put a heavy burden on himself generally. "I have a tremendous pressure to be successful," he stated. "Sometimes," he concluded, "I have even felt like running away, but where do you hide from a thing like this?"

Indeed, where do you hide? The rhythm of male life may vary, but success—money, position and image—steadfastly remains a priority at all levels. Men from diverse geographic regions and across socioeconomic strata, time after time intertwined the friendship experience with "who's on top, who's on bottom?" To most, life seemed to be about dividing men into winners and losers. Very few seemed to escape feeling one or the other and most felt like both at different times, during which they realized that although winning is sweet, it is the pain and agony of losing to another man which they feared above all.

Two researchers, Linden L. Nelson and Spencer Kagan, in a study published in *Psychology Today* (September 1972), provide evidence on this point. They found that a sample of youngsters on the West Coast consistently failed in their strivings for a series of rewards. Their lack of success was not due to personal deficiency but to overzealous competitive spirit in a situation where cooperation was required. So enmeshed were they in rivalry, most youngsters gave up their own prospects of success in order to deprive their fellow participants of prizes. The intensity of competitive behavior, it was found, increased with age. The older the child, the more likely he was to put aside personal benefit in favor of crushing his "adversary."

Comparing their West Coast findings with youngsters from other cultures, Nelson and Kagan found that the competitive spirit is not a global phenomenon. Mexican children, for example, were far more successful at the same tasks assigned American children. They were significantly more cooperative, did not become embroiled in dog-eat-dog conflicts and even avoided competition when it was to their benefit to do so. Nelson and Kagan suggest that the cross-cultural differences they identified were due to the dissimilar manner in which American and Mexican parents dispense approval. Mexican parents reward their children for effort; American parents gave rewards only for success. The Mexican children, less pressured to succeed, were able to be friendlier and more cooperative: They submitted to their rivals hoping that someone would win. The American children, in contrast, had learned that in order to be recognized, success was mandatory. Thus, they persisted in bitter rivalry to the end: "Ha, ha, now you won't get a toy!" Obviously, the American approach creates a "paranoid" distance between people. Looking behind, at the side and above as one climbs the success ladder, to see if a rival is gaining or toppling, does nothing for empathy—a key ingredient to close personal relations.

Self-Disclosure versus Self-Enclosure

As Roger Nichols (quoted earlier) found, women often facilitated personal conversation among men. An example frequently spoken of was the woman in a mixed group who makes a personal reference, thereby breaking the ice for a more intimate discussion. Some men at this point give each other a familiar look and retreat to "male talk":

Gregg: Yeah, I saw that game. They looked like shit.
Jeff: The hell they did. Those guys have been playing their asses off all season.
Gregg: (Forcefully) Well, one way or another, they lost it.
Jeff: They may have lost but they played a hell of a game. They shouldn't have lost by twenty points. Just bad luck.
Mike: (Grinning smugly) It's not just bad breaks. They would've played better at home. All that ass in the stands, cheering for them, that can take any guy off the disabled list.

While some men shy away from personal conversation even under female safeguard (or because of it), others, seeing an opportunity to loosen their strongly felt restraint against self-disclosure, leap in. As one man admitted in a drunken confidence: "Since I am talking to the women instead of the men, it feels more acceptable. I don't feel like I'm violating the male norm or something."

The ill effects of the inhibition of self-disclosure are far-reaching. It has even been suggested by Dr. Sidney Jourard, psychologist and researcher, that the male constraint may be an important factor in their lowered life expectancy. Low self-disclosure also has been identified as a factor in depression, anxiety, loneliness and marital strife as well as the high incidence of suicide among men. In any case, the male prohibition on self-disclosure makes it extraordinarily difficult to move closer to other men.

Like the majority of men, Herb Green had been brought up to cherish the necessity and importance of putting all his energies into his work. He was fully committed to the virtues of achievement and did not understand why he was so depressed. In his diligence to rise higher on the corporate ladder, he did not notice that he had gradually distanced himself from friends and co-workers; he had boxed himself into a world without people. As it is with most men, he sought therapy only when he was almost at bottom; he had concluded he was some kind of pariah, unlikable though he honestly could not understand why. Eight months after beginning group therapy, he speaks of his experience with other men:

"Until I started group, I didn't really think another man would be interested in my feelings. I thought it was—this sounds bizarre—'sissy-type behavior.' I considered it babyish, unmanly. I felt other men would surely see it the same way and be turned off by me. The message I got growing up, even from my best friends in high school, was: Show any weakness and we'll clobber you with it. Certainly, corporate work did nothing to dispel that; in the boardroom qualities of the head are rewarded, not the heart. Through group therapy I have become closer to men, but even there, ironically, a lot of competition is evident. God help you if you don't get in touch with your feelings quickly. There's still a race to be first and best even with feelings. I also notice that a few of the men play at being open—they take the role of analyst rather than revealing themselves. This contributes to my distrust of other men, and one of these days I'm going to work up the courage to confront these guys. I haven't progressed that far yet. I also haven't found a real friend, someone I can confide in and completely trust. But now I'm looking, I'm much more open to it. I would really like to have a buddy, someone I can be open with."

Another man, a middle-aged university professor, when asked

about the closeness of his male friendships and the nature of his interactions with other men, shared these observations of himself and his colleagues: "I work at being open with other men; I don't find it easy. As a child I remember doing things with my friends, being active not talkative. We went camping, played basketball, built clubhouses, that sort of thing. My attention was drawn not to what people thought or felt, but what we or they were doing. If someone chose my company I assumed he liked me; it was never discussed. When I was rejected or slighted, I felt hurt; just as liking was not a topic of discussion, neither was dislike. Of course I had feelings about my friends and I assumed they had feelings about me, but relationships were taken for granted, not analyzed. I can't remember a single instance of even considering a discussion of personal feelings—how I really felt about some-thing—especially about another person, until I was in graduate school and developed a close friendship.

"As for other men I come in contact with on campus—students and faculty—I see some bright spots among the young men, par-ticularly those in humanities and social sciences. But for the most part it appears as though the inhibitions I experienced as a younger man have continued through the adult life of many of my contem-poraries. Their conversations say it all. I hardly ever hear men use themselves as examples, their talk is impersonal. They talk about everything but people and how they are affected by others. It's the same old story, much of the interaction sounds like a news broadcast: impersonal, detached, distant. Everything is dis-cussed as if it had no real emotional connection. The few subjects which are controversial, which border on the personal (job insecurity, tenure, pressure to publish), are shaped into abstract, intellectual issues. A guy who is scared shit his position is in jeopardy because of a paucity of publications will initiate a dis-cussion on 'Teacher Competence versus Ability to Churn Out Research as a Basis for Promotion.' Head shit! The political issues of the day are another discussion mainstay. That seems to be meaty and safe enough to be kicked about endlessly."

The views of 168 college students and faculty members strongly support this professor's casual impression. Asked to describe their favored male heroes in an exploratory study prior to introducing the survey, they invariably wrote of men who were solitary, impersonal and actively working to overcome obstacles to the achievement of material success. Rarely were their heroes in search of closer relationships with other people.

A number of men wrote of suddenly becoming aware of their isolation and their lack of intimacy with other men when they reached a crisis in their life. Eliot Teller, a mature man of forty-eight, married and the father of three children, had such an awakening. His wife had been in the hospital for a few weeks with both emotional and physical problems when he was informed by her physician that her condition had deteriorated, lowering her chances for recovery very substantially. In a word, she was dying.

"What I felt like doing was calling a buddy. 'Hey, I'm hurting, patch me up!' But I didn't know whom to call. I felt as if a truck just shoved its way into my gut and suddenly I became aware of how isolated I had become in marriage. I had no friends. My single friends had drifted away after my marriage. Now we seemed a solar system apart. I had acquaintances, not friends. Dinner-party acquaintances, business acquaintances, neighbors, a sports freak or two, but no real buddy. Nobody I felt comfortable turning to."

Eliot went through the list. There was his architect friend who seemed to be building skyscrapers in his head the last time they talked and who was into giving him a Dunn and Bradstreet report on his success. Brendan was a colleague, not a friend. He saw Arnold at hockey games. The deepest conversation they ever had was on the strengths and weaknesses in the New York Rangers' first line. Fred, recently married, was still into one-night stands. He was making the rounds of singles' bars, checking into a "fuck motel" for a few hours and drifting home to his justifiably suspicious wife. Ralph, Eliot's younger brother, was never a buddy.

The only time he made contact was when he had a crazy business scheme and no cash. This simply served as a reminder that he still hadn't learned to wipe his own ass, he was still the kid who needed to be bailed out. He was not an equal to be counted on.

There were buddies in the old neighborhood and in college and people from various jobs who were friends for a while, but they were gone. Eliot had confined himself to a cluster of similarly married couples with whom small talk was the order of the day. He had put everything into his marriage and nothing into his friendships. There was not another man he regularly talked to. Finally, he put all his thoughts on paper. He just sat and wrote what was in his head and heart, and he felt somewhat relieved but, as Eliot expressed it, "There was no feedback. There was no one clued into me well enough to really understand. It's funny, because I was sure I had lots of friends I could turn to in an emergency."

A Slap on the Back, Never a Hug

When a man is cooperative and emotionally expressive with other men, his behavior is often interpreted by these men as yielding. Yielding is considered weak, weakness is equated with being a sissy. A sissy is the opposite of everything manly, everything strong. European men have hugged and kissed each other for centuries. American men, in contrast, choose the more reserved handshake, the rugged slap on the back or poke in the ribs. It is not, as most of us would guess, primarily a fear of homosexuality that restrains men. To be sure, most men would not want to be labeled gay, but they are enlightened enough to know that homosexuality is a sexual preference, not something evident from appearance. Their concern is not with preference, it is with image. They do not want to appear unmanly.

Athletics are one of the few areas where men have permitted each other to touch and be touched through the ritual of swats across the behind and bear hugs without fearing for their image.

In fact, in these settings—football for instance—the sporting activity is considered so masculine that all doubt is canceled. It is like saying, in effect, "I've got masculinity to spare. I am very sure of myself." Just as physical affection is masked by athletics or alcohol (picture the familiar scene of two drunks holding each other up), verbal expression is similarity disguised. Men often spoke of greeting each other with something like "hey, you old fuck" as a sign of flattery, a statement of their affection. They may buy drinks for a buddy or go out on a limb, but rarely is "I really like you" uttered. Again, it is considered unmanly.

One pattern found in interviews that may be related to the high priority given the masculine image is the infrequency with which two men get together without a specific, task-oriented agenda. Men get together for sporting activities, to conduct business, to play cards, to drink and so on. Only occasionally did two men meet (except after a prolonged absence) just to talk; men expressed more comfort in groups—presumably because the intensity of feelings is defused by the crowd. Personal communication, which was characterized by one man as "giving in to your feelings" is more difficult in the group setting and is traded, with a sigh of relief, for a commodity of higher value: mutual reassurance of masculinity.

A thirty-six-year-old stockbroker was particularly expressive on the issue of masculinity: "I have a feeling that appearing unmasculine is a burning, hidden issue with a lot of men. Put a straight man in a room alone with another man purported to be gay and I think you'll find that heterosexual men literally panic. All you have to do is look around you. Women kiss each other when they meet; men are uncomfortable with an arm around their shoulders, even a close friend's—the only exceptions I've noticed are when they are drunk or there's been a real crisis. These occasions, and of course sports, are excused. In other instances, onlookers might misinterpret what they saw or, even worse, the men themselves may question their masculinity."

This same man, when urged to be more personal, to speak of

his interaction with other men, shared this: "When I was growing up my dad hugged and kissed my sister and played rough with my brother and me. There was a time when I was openly affectionate and physically demonstrative with my brother (I had kissed him on the lips) and I sensed strong vibrations of disapproval from my father. I remember his saying men shake hands, they don't kiss. He seemed really upset. Soon, the thought of being hugged or kissed by another man—occasionally by my uncle, for example—would send shivers down my spine. By seven or eight I felt embarrassed and resentful if I were treated that way—especially in front of peers! The message was powerful and clear: Affection between 'real' men was to be disguised through aggression. A mock punch, an underhanded compliment: 'If you weren't such a snake with the women, I'd have you meet my wife'—that sort of thing. Despite my conditioning, which I have become aware of in the last couple of years—I credit that to the Women's Movement—I am starting to loosen up a bit. Women have told me that the men they know have very few close friends. That was, I realized, my experience as well. It's not that I don't know a lot of men. I do. It's more that my relationships with men are impersonal. I'm not happy with this and lately I've made an effort to articulate my feelings as they arise in the context of my male relationships. I often find that they are shared by others, although on several occasions the air was heavy with anxiety—mine as well as theirs."

That some men can question themselves about being intimate with friends—physically close with friends—that it can be seen as a positive behavior to be valued rather than shunned, is a very encouraging sign. Most men acknowledge, in in-depth interviews, the difficulty of easing up on their masculine image. Their apprehension was firm but amorphous; they knew they would feel vulnerable but could not discern why. Some feared rejection by other males; others equated appearing unmasculine with failure. Many vaguely intuited an unexplored void and did not press further. They felt safer simply keeping up a strong front—"I can never know whether my feelings are shared by other men or whether I'm just too sensitive," one man said.

Connections: Active, Convenient, Advisory, Intense

The majority of men may not have close friends, but they do not conduct their lives in isolation. Most—almost three-quarters of the sample—have a variety of valued same-sex relationships. These include activity friends, convenience friends and mentor friends. An activity friend may be a weekly tennis partner, a drinking buddy, a man (or group of men) sharing the same hobby. The relationship is not likely to be deep nor need it be, it is companionable and usually a much-needed outlet. Convenience friends have a relationship based on the exchange of favors —you drive me to work and I'll help you fix the lawnmower. This is the man to be called when something must be borrowed; he lives close by or is a coworker. Frequently he is the other half of a couple in which the wives are close friends. Convenience friends afford each other practical assistance. Seldom do men in these relationships form strong emotional connections; they know little of one another and prefer a limited arrangement.

A mentor friendship contains strong emotion but it is not a relationship among equals; rather it occurs between a younger and an older man. The mentor is ordinarily looked up to as someone who is accomplished in a field the younger man aspires to; he has been where the younger man wants to go and is able to offer direction, welcoming the initiate into a new occupational or social world.

"Harold gave me tremendous support and encouragement. I was very close to this man—enormously and deeply affected by him in fact. He really taught me how to doctor, how to pick up subtle diagnostic signals in a patient, how to conduct a practice and to be cognizant of the politics of medicine. We saw each other socially, played golf together, but medicine was the foundation of our relationship. He had an unusual commitment to medicine and was very willing to give of himself. I realized later that this quality was offered only as long as I remained a novice. As the balance of giving/receiving became more equal, our relationship became more distant. Our friendship is more mutual now. I'm as likely to give him advice as he is me. But I no longer experience the intimacy we once shared."

The mentor relationship, as in this instance, may cool off as the two men become equals; it may come to a natural end as the men drift apart. Sometimes it ends bitterly as the younger man seeks to liberate himself in a manner reminiscent of a father-son independence struggle and, occasionally, the pair may form a warm, moderately close friendship.

Although male friendships are often slow to develop due to the wariness with which men regard each other, a gradual shift has been taking place in recent years. Those men who have begun to share parenting responsibilities, who have been influenced by the women's movements to redefine their roles, have become less fiercely competitive, more able to recognize and share their feelings and, consequently, better candidates for solid friendships. This transition, I discovered, is most prominent in men who are in their mid-thirties. In fact, nearly ninety percent of males reporting close friendships were in their thirties or older. During his late teens, twenties and early thirties, a man's primary concern is his career and the establishment of a home base, a family. It is in his mid to late thirties that these stirrings stabilize and he is apt to experience, most acutely, his loneliness. By this age he has had ample time to mature, to feel reasonably established, and is less needful of proving his masculinity than the younger man; he is more open at mid-age to a close connection than his youthful counterpart.

It is perhaps a lack of developmental readiness that accounts, at least in part, for the lack of real friendship ties in situations which seem ready-made for lifelong commitment between men —the combat-buddy relationship, for instance. It is commonly assumed that these circumstances create strong, lasting bonds.

Our images focus on men saving each other's lives, mourning each other's deaths, forming business partnerships after the war's over. When examined closely, the emotional bond is largely mythical in origin. Of sixty-two ex-servicemen interviewed, only seven could say they even saw any of their old buddies. Carl, a thirty-year-old Vietnam veteran, explained:

"It's not like in the movies, you know, guys sticking together because of real liking for each other. I had buddies but it was to help you get through the night—basic survival. We were not really that personally close, only committed to watch out for each other. You couldn't afford to be too close. And you couldn't afford to be choosey. Your very life depended on how quickly another man—a stranger, or someone you might not even like in ordinary circumstances—reacted. Being too personal, being too upset when a 'friend' dies, gets in the way. It's dangerous. The ultimate goal was to be untouched by that, to keep functioning, to come out in one piece. Making friends was not a real consideration. A buddy, quite simply, was *any* guy who knew his job and kept you alive."

Reflecting on his combat experience, one man, although basically in agreement with Carl's assessment, added an important point: "Many men, particularly the younger ones, broke down in front of other men. This was a painful scene all around. The man who witnesses the emotional upset senses his own weaknesses and rather than feeling sympathy wants to shut the experience out." Being raised to "tough it out" and being at an age when this strategy is at a premium makes seeing old buddies an agonizing reminder of past vulnerabilities which many men feel are better left behind. Sociologist Rex Lucas, in his book *Men In Crisis*, draws a parallel to the male combat experience. Lucas describes a group of miners entombed in a caved-in mine for eight days. Before their rescue they cried in front of each other and supported each other; they depended on each other for their very existence. These men could not, in a physical or psychological sense, have been closer during their ordeal. Yet, six months later, Lucas asserts, they were embarrassed if they encountered each other for any length of time.

In the work setting, another mythical stronghold of male camaraderie, my investigation once again challenged conventional belief. Most men protected themselves from the corrosive effects of rivalry by purposely avoiding friendships on the job. In effect, they did not want to continue a relationship that was already strongly competitive. This was most true of executives—those in the most competitive kinds of positions—who indicated almost unanimously that they preferred to form relationships with persons in organizations or professions other than their own. The few exceptions came from men who were either well established or in organizations described as noncompetitive. Practically all were above age thirty-five.

In sum, those men that do unite in a close relationship are approaching mid-life and do not work under the same roof. Predictably, they share similar interests and have a common value system. Sometimes, they meet while undergoing crucial times together; a divorce experience, a bout with alcoholism, a financial setback or the like. Most often, mutual recreational or work interests—and occasionally, a mutual acquaintance—bring them into contact and the chemistry, a factor which defies analysis, is highly compatible. One such relationship, that of Hank Evanston and Paul Carter, notable for its intensity and passion, is recounted:

"My friend Paul had been a painter, actor, photographer, writer and troublemaker. We met through a mutual acquaintance who felt we would be drawn to each other. I, too, was involved in the arts and had my share of trouble. My first meeting with Paul confirmed what I had been told about him. He was a marvel, a man with an inner glow and eyes that danced with playfulness; a witty man with enormous charm. His temperament was by turns tough and tender. He had this fundamentally twinkly attitude. I remember watching him walk. There was something about his movement; he was sure, deliberate; he was a man who pushed himself to the limits and had somehow survived—you could get that from his presence. He was not a timid or apologetic man. He was not ashamed to stand upright and say, 'This is me, contradictions, foibles and all.'

"That first summer we found ourselves having dinner together as often as twice a week. The friendship grew intimate in bounds. Neither of us was one to stand on ceremony. Oft times, we were inseparable. Over the next few years we walked the nighttime streets of many cities, talking of our future, women, careers, the meaning of life. He was sometimes surprisingly inarticulate for a writer, but he insisted that one talk about one's own feelings. When I tended to get overly intellectual, he would keep pulling me back. He'd say, 'But what does it mean to you? How do you feel about it? What's your involvement?' Paul was also extremely direct. He dared to display emotions I had felt—feelings that seemed to be denied among my associates. We drank together, we'd walk along the beach together, we'd swim together. There was a certain kind of roughhousing to our relationship, a kind of playfulness and male camaraderie. But there was no fear of affection, there was a side of our relationship that was very loving and tender. It was one of the most open relationships I remember having with another man; between bouts of trading punches and wrestling, there was a strong mutual admiration, great affection. We loved each other."

After several years of association, Paul journeyed to the West Coast in search of his dream: to be a successful screenwriter. The two men continued their bond, faithfully writing each other. After a while, though, Hank ceased hearing from Paul. His letters went unanswered; Paul's phone number had been changed and unlisted. Almost a year passed without a word—but not for want of trying. A trip to California proved futile. Paul had left his apartment without a forwarding address. He had dropped out of sight. So far as Hank knew, Paul did not see or correspond with anyone he knew from his days in New York. Hank was at a complete loss to explain what had happened until one day he found Paul waiting on tables in a Greenwich Village restaurant.

His life had fallen apart, his dream was crushed. The loneliness of Los Angeles and the weight of his rejection slips had poisoned him. Hank continues:

"At that very moment I understood his disappearance. But how can you tell an old friend that you understand his harsh disappointment, that failure has sometimes infected your spirit too and that you like him anyway, that he's still a buddy? Do you just say you don't care a damn whether he's realized his dream, he's still an important part of the human community? Do you tell him that you sympathize with his unspoken embarrassment and understand his painful confrontation with his limits? This would be such an affront to Paul, such a condescending insult to this proud man, an enormous assault on his effort to maintain his dignity. Instead, I hugged him and shed a tear with him. That was enough. In time we were able to talk and to resume our friendship. Gradually we overcame the barriers of failed ambition. Our friendship, once again, became as it had been—even richer."

The following year, twelve years and two weeks after they had met, Paul died suddenly of a heart attack. It was a terrible shock for Hank. The funeral intensified his awareness of how important Paul had been to him. Hank concludes: "When I heard of Paul's death, my whole life up to that point went before my eyes. I could not control, nor did I try to control my grief. I hadn't really cried that way since I was a child. Paul was a part of my life, the best and the purest part. He brought me warmth, hope, trust and generosity. I learned from Paul the courage to be me. I appreciated his comeback after the horror of the Los Angeles years; he renewed himself and was able, once more, to laugh at life's adversities. This was a man of courage. He was my spiritual brother. We saw things the same way. He knew what I was thinking and I knew what he was thinking. We had traveled together, played together, drunk wine, strolled beaches and city streets together. We cried together and opened our lives to each other. I miss him dearly."

Amid the many accounts of male-male hostility and competition in all walks of life—from the corporate board room to the fields of war—relationships such as Hank and Paul's offer a reminder: There are enriching male friendships, relationships of mutual trust, respect and protectiveness. Some men are tender with each other; they are capable of putting aside rivalry and mourning the misfortune of other men. These are the men who, in their survey responses and follow-up interviews, spoke of truly enjoying the company and friendships of other men; they related feelings of relaxation; finding it less important to censor their thoughts and feelings, they felt more spontaneous in each other's presence, felt freer to ask favors and to do favors. They trusted each other. As one man explained, "We have incorporated ourselves, my friend and I, into each other's psyche." These men took the risks and losses that make for solidarity, at whatever price, with others of their own sex.

Myth, Reality and Shades of Gray: Comparing Same-Sex Friendships

THE PHYSICAL DIFFERENCES between men and women are obvious and universal. As for differences related to sex roles, each society varies in this, as Margaret Mead has convincingly demonstrated. Dr. Mead showed that in three New Guinea tribes, there was considerable difference from tribe to tribe in masculine and feminine behavior. In one group, the Arapesh, men and women alike were passive, "maternal," cooperative and nonaggressive. In the Mundugumor, a tribe in geographic proximity to the Arapesh, men and women alike were fierce, cruel and aggressive. A third tribe, the Tchambuli, showed yet another pattern of sex typing. The men were passive, dependent individuals who spent their time cultivating the arts while the women took the more active, assertive role of provider.

In America, most researchers concede that boys and girls are

78

brought up in divergent ways, taught different skills, rewarded for diverse acts. Women, it is agreed, excel at certain tasks, men at others. There is little argument that some personality traits appear more dominant in one sex than the other. All of this not-withstanding, sex differences are a hotly contested issue—from occupational controversy to debates about the Equal Rights Amendment—masculine and feminine behavior is very much in the media these days. Since the rise of the women's movement, sex-role behavior has come under closer scrutiny. How has this affected friendship? How do the sexes differ in their friendship relations? Drawing from the findings of the two preceding chap-ters, some dimensions of the same-sex friendship experience are compared below.

Early Impressions. Most preteen children have a best friend who is usually someone of the same sex and similar age. Both sexes share an essentially positive recollection of these childhood friendships; they do not differ in this respect. However, the type of play engaged in during these early friendships is telling of the divergence to come: Boys tend to form play groups that are competitive in nature; girls' groups more frequently revolve around cooperative enterprises. Thus, at an early age, boys be-come concerned with trying hard and winning while girls, by contrast, play house and school, engaging in roles that require complementary support.

Speaking of their childhood, men recall being highly respon-sive to and aware of the sex-role opinions of other boys. Girls in preteen years appear to be less susceptible to sex-role pressure. While "sissy" is the most powerful charge against the young male ego, prior to puberty girls do not report sensitivity to accu-sations that they are being unfeminine. It is not until the dating years, when competition for boys becomes an issue, that women report being concerned with feminine behavior. Males, for the most part, are responsive to the suggestion that their behavior is unmanly at almost any age.

These early attitudes, reinforced by social conditioning, continue to play an active part in the friendships of both sexes during adolescence. This is a period when the majority of males once again report a close alliance with same-sex friends but now, with heightened intensity, considerable energy is devoted to jockeying for position and a definite undercurrent of competition pervades the relationship. Although in dissimilar fashion, females share equally fragile relationships at this age. For them the bond of loyalty extends only to the line of romantic involvement. This is most apt to be the case in late adolescence, when dating and relationships with boys take sharp precedence over sisterhood. Actually, dating dilutes the intensity of same-sex friendships for men also. For the majority of us—men and women alike—the moment we begin to date seriously, there is a competition between romance and friendship. Add to this career strivings and family obligations, and close friendships move to the back burner. It isn't until our third decade that they are once again revived.

Getting Personal. Male friendships revolve almost exclusively around work and play: The office or the assembly line, the hobby or sports activity, these are the focal areas of friendship talk. Most notable about male friendships is that they rarely include personal, confidential exchanges. Men who have known each other for years may not know anything about each other's family crises or problems.

Women, unlike men, do use their friendships to share difficult times and to ask for help. Their friendships have a decidedly personal flavor; women are nearly three times more likely than men to have a close confidante. Even though self-disclosure is an infrequent occurrence, it is clear that men desire others with whom to share problems and personal experiences. Those men who do fulfill this longing are more likely to turn to a woman or a stranger than to each other. Women, on the other hand, practically always choose a same-sex friend. Individuals of either sex who have a trusted friend to whom they can express thoughts, feelings and opinions honestly are less likely to report symptoms of depression and loneliness than those who do not have the benefit of this experience.

This is not to say that the sheer amount of self-disclosure that goes on between friends is an index of the health of the relationship or of the persons. There are such factors as timing, interest of the other person, appropriateness and the effects of the disclosures on either party which also must be considered. If a relationship exists between self-disclosure and factors of psychological health, research trends suggest it is curvilinear, not linear; that is, too much disclosure and too little disclosure may be associated with undesirable symptoms, while some intermediate amount, under appropriate conditions, is related to a sense of well-being.

While very high self-disclosure is not necessarily a blessing, as a general principle most of us agree that never knowing what a companion really thinks, feels and wants is distressing and quite unpleasant. This guardedness is a dominant theme in male interaction; it is, by comparison, a minor issue among women. In short, women as a group demonstrate substantially more trust than do men.

Attractions and Hazards. Such qualities of a relationship as openness, compassion and mental stimulation are of concern to most of us regardless of sex, but—judging from the questionnaire response—they are more important to women than to men. Asked to consider the ingredients of close friendship, women rated these qualities above all others. Men assigned a lower priority to them in favor of similarity in interests, selected by seventy-seven percent of men, and responsiveness in a crisis, chosen by sixty-one percent of male respondents. Mental stimulation, ranked third in popularity by men as well as women, was the only area of overlap. Among men, only twenty-eight percent named openness as an important quality; caring was picked by just twenty-three percent.

It is evident by their selections that when women speak of

close friendships they are referring to emotional factors, while men emphasize the pleasure they find in a friend's company. That is, when a man speaks of "a friend" he is likely to be talking about someone he does things with—a teammate, a fellow hobbyist, a drinking buddy. These activities are the fabric of the friendship; it is a "doing" relationship in which similarity in interests is the key bond. This factor was a consideration of a meager eleven percent of women. Women opt for a warm, emotional atmosphere where communication flows freely; activity is mere background.

Lastly, men, as we have seen, have serious questions about each other's loyalty. Perhaps this is why they placed such strong emphasis on responsiveness in a crisis—"someone I can call on for help." Women, as their testimonies indicate, are generally more secure with each other and consequently are more likely to treat this issue lightly. In follow-up interviews this was confirmed numerous times as woman after woman indicated that "being there when needed was taken for granted."

As for the hazards of friendship, more than a few relationships have been shattered because of cutthroat competition and feelings of betrayal. This applies to both men and women, but unequally. In comparison, nearly twice as many men complained about these issues as women. Further, while competition and betrayal are the main thorns to female friendship, men are plagued in almost equal amounts by two additional issues: guardedness (lack of candor) and a fear of appearing unmanly. Obviously, for a man, a good friend is hard to find.

Friendships: Desire, Quality and Source. The literature on sex differences is replete with discussions of the greater affiliative and nurturant needs of women and the greater male needs for independence, achievement and aggression. Curiously enough, although men and women do react to the friendship experience differently, their desires for companionship are of similar intensity. As mentioned earlier, both men and women in their twenties consider friendship to play a relatively minor role in their lives.

This, as might be predicted, is less true for single individuals than it is for those who are married. Nonetheless, there is no significant distinction to be made with regard to males and females. The friendship desires of men and women beyond the late twenties are once again congruent but are increased in comparison to their younger counterparts—sixty-two percent of men and sixty-seven percent of women over age twenty-nine consider friendship to play a moderately important part in their lives, as compared to twenty-eight percent of younger men and thirty-one percent of younger women.

Men and women may assess the role of friendship in their lives similarly, but the extent of their actual friendships varies considerably. Among my respondents, adult women (over age twenty) were at least twice as likely as adult men to have a close friend. The conventional belief that of the two sexes, men have the richer friendships is simply untrue. The only exception to this may be in regard to mentor relationships in the work setting. Although the questionnaire did not cover this topic, interview impressions are that women as a group have less mentor relationships than men. The scarcity of women in high-level positions possibly accounts for this. In general, though, women as a group are less frustrated, more in tune with their friendship goals than are men. Other friendship researchers agree: Dr. Alan Booth of the University of Nebraska studied the friendship patterns of eight hundred adults in two major cities and found that both working-class and middle-class women had more solid and emotionally satisfying friendships than did working-class and middle-class men. In another investigation, Dr. Mirra Komarovsky scrutinized a number of blue-collar marriages and found that six out of every ten wives she interviewed, but only two out of every ten husbands, enjoyed close nonfamilial relationships.

Just as the extent and quality of close friendships differ between the sexes, so do their sources of friendship. Employed activity attracts many women as much for the companionship and friendship to be found on the job as for the work or money earned. Men, more influenced by on-the-job competition, avoid friendships in this setting. Instead, they form relationships with persons in similar work but different organizations or through mutual recreational interests and men's clubs. Men more than women are apt to be of the same ages and, as already noted, have the same interests. Single men are more likely than single women to join company exclusively with other singles. Men more than women have educational backgrounds in common with their friends.

Implications. Clearly, the two sexes travel a different friendship path. If an atmosphere of discovery and delight pervades many female friendships, an atmosphere of ambivalence is the most generous characterization that can be ascribed to the state of male relationships. Because they have been exposed to sex roles that are constraining and dysfunctional, men have allowed themselves precious few options for friendship. Generation upon generation of boys (and girls) have been presented with male role models who have an inexhaustible capacity to withstand not only adversity and pain, but any feeling.

From Hercules to James Bond, the heroic man is presented as impenetrable. Witness some discriminating reactions to male and female children: A shy little girl is considered cute; a shy boy is thought of as a sissy. A frightened girl is comforted; a boy is admonished to act like a man. Girls are allowed comfortably to kiss each other and to cry openly without shame; boys who even touch each other had better be "horsing around," and crying is done only at the expense of sheer ridicule.

These behavioral distinctions, which may seem extreme to some, were confirmed in a recent study commissioned by the United States government. It was revealed that the majority of tested parents would not hug or cuddle their sons (after the average age of five) as often as they did their daughters (regardless of age), would not kiss male children at all after a certain age (usually the onset of adolescence), and would discourage boys as young as four years old from sobbing by calling them crybabies or telling them to "act their age." When asked to explain, the most common response from the parents was: "I don't want my son to grow up to be a sissy."

Without doubt, women have also had their difficulties with rigid sex-role training. If men have been told that rough and tough is masculine, women have been told that soft and sweet is feminine. Rather than seeing themselves as full human beings capable of versatile roles, many women have confined themselves to one dimension: Mother, Companion, Follower, Bitch, Homemaker, Whore, Glamor Girl. Unrealistic views such as these wreak havoc on friendship relations.

It may come down to this: When men or women confine themselves exclusively to either "masculine" or "feminine" behavior, they are being incomplete human beings. The inevitable result is that their friendships prove to be unsatisfactory. The psychologically healthy individual, one who is able to develop satisfying, nurturing relationships, must be nonconforming in this respect. He or she is a person who takes the relatively fixed sex roles in our society and redefines them in ways that dovetail better with his or her needs. Consequently, he or she has greater freedom to express and act out a wider range of feelings and behavior. The benefits that men derive from sharing office or hobby interests could well be of value to women, while men could profit by learning to confide in each other about problems they find emotionally baffling. Healthy men and women can do many things that might be deemed "out of role" by some, and yet they need not experience any threat to their humanity—nor to their femininity or masculinity. They may cry, be tender, touch, ask for help as well as be independent, assertive and ambitious.

Friendship Between Men and Women: In Body and Spirit

The Sex War

WE HAVE SEEN that as a group neither males nor females live up to their friendship reputations; men are not nearly as chummy as supposed; women, accused of being fickle and underhanded, in actuality share substantial trust and mutual involvement. But what of the friendships between the sexes? To judge from societies that have existed previous to ours, the lives of men and women intersected rarely—at mealtime and bedtime. Historically, the pattern of relationships between men and women was built on differences arising from their differing biological roles. In primitive times, for example, woman's slighter, less muscled physique and her childbearing functions usually restricted her to duties inside the family dwelling. There was a division of labor between the procuring of food and protection on the one hand, and the preparation of food and the care of the family on the other. Accordingly, men and women did not have much in common except their economic and child-producing partnership. The real alliances of each sex, history tells us, were with those of their own kind—imperfect as they may have been.

George Santayana, in his *Little Essays* published in 1920, stresses the indestructible obstacles to friendship between a man and a woman.

"Friends are generally of the same sex, for when men and women agree, it is only in their conclusions; their reasons are always different. So that while intellectual harmony between men and women is easily possible, its delightful magical quality lies precisely in the fact that it does not arise from mutual understanding, but is a conspiracy of alien essences and a kissing, as it were, in the dark. . . . Friendship with a woman is therefore apt to be more or less than friendship; less, because there is no intellectual parity; more, because (even when the relation remains wholly dispassionate, as in respect to old ladies) there is something mysterious and oracular about a woman's mind which inspires a certain instinctive deference and puts it out of the question to judge what she says by male standards. . . . This though not complete, as that which separates us from the dumb animals, is radically incompatible with friendship."

With the gradual progress of civilization, the emphasis on hunting shifted to the tilling of the soil and, with the domestication of animals, physical strength became less important. The coming of industrialization eliminated the hunt for food, and man's need to ward off enemies disappeared. Today, with more women in the work force and the increased leisure time available to many of us, men and women have unprecedented opportunities to interact. If lack of varied contact was an issue in the past, it is no longer of significant consequence. But an old story hinted at by Santayana endures: The Battle of the Sexes.

Beginning with the legend of Adam and Eve, continuing through the days of suffrage agitation and into modern struggles for equality, the relationships of men and women have been alloyed with irritation, rivalry and strife. The myths and prejudices surrounding male-female relations die hard. Though contemporary men and women often work side by side and may even wear similar apparel, this is no indication that all is harmonious; many are engaged in hand-to-hand combat. Consider these comments by male and female front-line soldiers.

A twenty-seven-year-old female accountant had this to say: "I had always assumed that I was an insider in our office. Maybe not one of the boys, but at least accepted and respected. At lunch one day though, after a couple of drinks the men began airing their grievances against women. I was the only woman present and they just ignored me; they acted as if I just wasn't there. They launched their attack knowing full well that they would have the support of each other: "Men need to work," it began; "women are a leisure class trespassing into an already tight job market." Here I was working as hard as any of them for a lower salary than the men in this position and they were complaining. I was mortified. The fear of competition from women was so pervasive that it was scary. I felt I had been duped into thinking I was accepted. More accurately, I was viewed as the enemy. They made that quite clear. Equal pay for women implies equal status, and that is just too threatening for men. If friendship is a relationship of equals, then men are not ready for it because they are not really acceptant of equality."

A (male) advertising executive, forty-six, angrily exclaimed: "Women automatically blame men as the cause of all their problems. Because they don't know what they want, they acquiesce, let men take responsibility—from picking up the restaurant tab to making important decisions—and then complain that they are being dominated. Caught by the double bind of wanting to be self-supporting and at the same time wanting to be taken care of, women send out conflicting messages to men: 'Come here . . . go away.' I very rarely meet a woman who can just hang loose and be herself."

A (female) hotel manager, forty-three, declared a contrary but equally strong position: "I don't hate men, but I don't count any among my real friends. There are several reasons for this, but one of the most important is that I don't experience a sense of authentic respect from men. Yes, they are polite and courteous. But often there is an undercurrent of dominance/submissiveness in these gestures. Chivalry has become a weapon in the male arsenal. The woman 'owes' a response. When expectations clash, the control element in chivalry becomes clear—'I took you out to dinner, treated you like a lady and now you are not going to invite me in?' Dominance over women is such an important part of the masculine ideal that men automatically fall into this role and are bewildered when they are confronted. Many male-female relationships have strong similarities to slave-master relationships —there is benevolence but not authentic respect as equals."

And this from a male postal clerk, fifty-one, who has been divorced four times: "I feel more comfortable talking about my troubles to women because I don't really care what they think of me."

A thirty-three-year-old (male) biology teacher felt women lacked identification with the male "psyche": "If I told a woman I ran a three-hour marathon, she would say, 'That's terrific.' She would probably support my effort but she wouldn't really understand what it means to run that well. Another man would know and appreciate what I'm talking about in a way a woman couldn't. Harry, for example, is a track coach. When he heard my time he came right over and congratulated me. He told me he would help me train for Boston. I don't know if I can keep it up, but I'm sure going to try. I was flying for a week after he told me that."

A (male) machinist, thirty-six, seemed fed up: "The conversations of women, because of the way they spend their time, are— let's face it—boring. Who wants to hear about triviality, gossip and daily humdrum."

A thirty-eight-year-old (female) personnel assistant felt similarly—but toward men: "Men are dull. Listen to them talk. One way or another they are trying to convince others (and themselves) that they are big deals. Men talk *to* women, not *with* them. A man's approach to a woman is almost invariably one of conquest, not of friendship; the strategy is to impress her with position, accomplishments and machismo; the goal, if not seduction, is to reaffirm that all's right with man and his world."

Lastly, a (female) computer programmer, thirty-six, offered a brief synopsis of the male-female conflict: "Women have been trying hard these days to get out from under the images that have been imposed on them. Men aren't in the same boat. I think they rather like their images. A great number of the men I know have an air of superiority about them in regard to women—they are still clinging to paternalist notions about women. This attitude allows them to feel safe around women. As long as men feel on top, they're feeling okay. When they encounter a woman who is attractive, openly intelligent and worldly, they frequently beat a hasty retreat. Because of this, most of the successful women I know do not have true friendships with men. They have lovers, older brother–kid sister relationships, but not friendships. Men suffer as much from this as women. They are bored with women who have bought the passive, dependent role, but they are so committed to the masculine image of superiority that they cannot open up enough to make real contact with a less traditional woman. They are unwilling to risk their image with anyone they can't control."

Although the opinions aired above may sound stark, they are not the stirrings of a bitter minority; over one-third of the male respondents and fifteen percent of the females interviewed expressed similar views—together they comprised nearly one-half of the interview sample. This is not atypical. As the social-science literature and numerous psychological surveys convincingly demonstrate, males and females are indoctrinated at an early age to view each other in sexist terms. In one study published in *Psychological Reports*, psychologist Ruth Hartley investigated the sex-role pressures of male children. The youngsters in Dr. Hartley's study described girls in the following way: "They have to stay close to the house; they are expected to play quietly and be gentler than boys; they are often afraid; they must not be rough; they have to keep clean; they cry when they are scared or hurt; they are afraid to go to rough places like rooftops or empty lots; their activities consist of 'fopperies' like playing with dolls, fussing over babies and sitting and talking about dresses; they need to know how to cook, sew and take care of children, but spelling and arithmetic are not as important for them as for boys."

Considering this characterization of females, it is not surprising that the boys in the Hartley study drew a sharply contrasting picture of themselves: "[Boys] have to be able to fight in case a bully comes along; they have to be athletic; they have to be able to run fast; they must be able to play rough games; they need to know how to play many games—curbball, baseball, basketball, football; they need to be smart; they need to be able to take care of themselves; they should know what girls don't know—how to climb, how to make a fire, how to carry things; they should have more ability than girls; they need to know how to stay out of trouble; they need to know arithmetic and spelling."

Here it is evident that boys don't see male and female roles as merely different. To be a male is clearly superior. Naturally, these youngsters do not consider adult status to affect any of this. They considered grown women to be, among other things, fearful, indecisive, unadventurous, uninteresting and more easily hurt and killed than men. They thought that women "have a way of doing things the wrong way." Of women's activities they said: "They are always at those crazy household duties and don't have time for anything else; their work is just regular drudging; women do things like cooking and washing and sewing because that's all they can do; women haven't enough strength in the head or in the body to do most jobs."

Men, by contrast, "mostly do what they want to do," decide how to spend the money and get first choice of the most comfortable chair. The result of this process, Dr. Hartley suggests, is "an overstraining to be masculine, a virtual panic at being caught doing anything traditionally defined as feminine, and hostility toward anything even hinting at 'femininity' including females themselves."

The position of women as not nearly the equal of men is hardly facilitative of friendship between the sexes. When women and men see each other in such stereotypical fashion, every encounter becomes heavy with unspoken demands: Confirm that I'm masculine (feminine); acknowledge that I'm desirable; prove to me that you recognize my equality (or superiority). Under these circumstances, when men and women meet only as potential competitors—lovers or enemies—rather than for a companionable exchange, tension and hostility prevail. Friendship doesn't stand a chance.

On the Sexual Front

While antagonism and prejudice drive men and women apart, lust draws them physically closer. As one woman stated, "If it [sex] is not center stage, you can bet it's lurking in the wings." Sexual feelings may be light or intense, in the background or on the surface, but they are always there. The importance of sex—though exaggerated by our culture—may encourage male-female alliances, but it just as often destroys a potentially satisfying friendship. Sexual questions create more of a conflict than many other issues in male-female friendships simply because we value sex so highly today. Sex promises everything—even if it doesn't always deliver: Emotional fulfillment, security, reassurance and intimacy top the list. In sexual matters our culture remains divided and confused. In truth, most of us are ambivalent about our sexuality with opposite-sex friends and do not know how to resolve the dilemma comfortably.

Some men and women resolve the dilemma neatly—they do not choose each other as friends. Others are so indiscriminately sexual that they shatter any hope of closeness with a single individual. These are the people—both married and unmarried—on a nearly ceaseless sexual hunt that expresses a complexity of feeling: lust, reassurance of worth and attractiveness, and perhaps the hope of finding a true love. They are in the market for romance, not friendship.

The double standard, diluted but still operative, is a factor here; men are more prone to sexual priorities and less comfortable with women when the relationship is intimate but nonsexual. The assumption that many men hold—"A real man with a man's penis will 'score' whenever possible"—places undue strain on friendship. In one notable example of this, the late President Johnson was suspected of having an affair with Doris Kearns—a friend and confidante who helped him deal with the contempt he faced from younger and academic people. Many observers assumed that there must be a sexual tie between these two, as if such intensity could not exist without sexual intimacy.

Women, too, fall victim to sexual pressures in their relationships with men. For them, questions of sexual involvement combine with unkind rumors to provoke a caution that is equally unsettling to friendship. The judgment—damned if you are yet more damned if you're not—is a familiar convolution for many women. Here, the expression of both men and women troubled by the predicament:

A twenty-nine-year-old (male) architect candidly remarked: "When I meet a good-looking woman and I don't come on to her sexually, I feel empty. It's not just that I missed an opportunity, it's more than that. I experience a sense of failure. I feel as if I am less of a man."

A bank executive, thirty-three, revealed her plan for coping with sexism: "I learned long ago that to be successful in a man's world requires that I be seen by my colleagues—both male and female—as asexual. My coworkers regard me as supercompetent, completely devoted to my work. Although I feel very womanly, I suppress every vestige of warmth and sexuality in favor of impersonal efficiency on the job. I dress conservatively, fix my hair purposely in a nonattractive manner and rarely wear makeup. The reason is simple: I don't pose the sexual challenge men practically always read into their relationships with women and therefore I am able to progress up the corporate ladder with fewer stumbling blocks. I am more or less accepted as 'one of the boys.' This makes it much easier for men to deal with me. Now, you see, they have a rationalization for belittling my success: 'She's a terrific executive, but I'll bet she hasn't had a good lay in years.' Actually, I dress differently and am quite sensual and sexual outside of work. It is only until most of the men at the office are my subordinates—which won't be too long—that I must remain 'in the closet.' After that, when I am in a position of power, my colleagues are going to have to learn real fast to take a sexy woman seriously."

And a thirty-two-year-old stockbroker spoke of a painful but enlightening occurrence: "I had an experience that cost me a potential friendship, but it opened my eyes to better relationships in the future. I had been spending the day with a woman who was introduced to me by a friend. This was a very bright, alive woman and most of the day was very pleasant; she was very companionable. Toward the late afternoon, we got into a terrifically heated argument about Marilyn French's novel *The Women's Room*. I thought it was a bitter, vicious attack on men, a very offensive hate manual. She felt it was a literary masterpiece filled with profound truths. After arguing for hours, she maneuvered me into a position where I literally had no response to her. I felt I had been outclassed by her; I felt defeated. When we got back to her apartment I wanted to run away, but instead I tried to force her to have sex with me. Although I wasn't desirous of sex at all—the afternoon wasn't particularly arousing for me—I pushed the issue. I felt beaten by the afternoon's debate and I was using sex to regain control. Needless to say, she no longer talks to me. It never really dawned on me before that dramatic—and traumatic—occurrence how much I view women not as people, but as sex objects."

From a twenty-six-year-old literary agent, a distressing experience which left her saddened and bitter: "We were such good friends, I even told him about the men in my love life—my romantic relationships—but after a few months he asked me to sleep with him. 'If I slept with other men, men I didn't even feel that close to,' he argued, 'why couldn't I sleep with him?' I was hurt. I knew it wasn't me he was interested in; he had just used a slower, more subtle strategy to get into my pants . . . we said goodbye."

An actress, forty-three, boldly discussed her sexual feelings: "Sexuality is always an issue with me. I don't want to be treated like a sister by a man. If I find a man attractive, I would be put off if he didn't want a sexual relationship. I would think he finds me unappealing. The only relationship with a man in which I could really relax would be with someone I knew to be homosexual. For example, recently when my husband was away on business, his friend Peyton, who is homosexual, came over. We related to each other completely unself-consciously because the sexual question was a nonissue. Now, when I am around Barry, even though it is clearly understood that sexual relations are completely outside the framework of our relationship, there is a tension—and it is specifically sexual. Our society focuses so heavily on the sexual side of life that it is very hard to forget. The sexual elements inhibit me, they distract me from really pursuing a friendship. The sexual signals are always there—they occur directly but more often they are flashing on the most delicate, most indirect level—as warnings to be careful, be alert. 'Watch out how this is interpreted, what did he mean by that, are we fooling ourselves, sublimating our romantic interests?'— these are all questions that nag at me when I'm interacting more intensely with an attractive man."

A forty-nine-year-old landscaper who had all but written off friendships with women explained: "I would like to have friendships with women; there's a whole range of emotions that can be tapped in these relationships, but it never works out. Either I'm sexually attracted and do not want 'just' friendship or I'm not really attracted and she's offended or suspicious of me. One way or another, though, the sexual issues takes precedence over everything else."

In our culture, as the individuals quoted above bear witness to, we have overemphasized the separation of the sexes and the pursuit of sexual fulfillment. Men and women together in a bond of friendship are suspect: Is one homosexual? Are they having an affair? Is he impotent? Although our respondents indicate these to be nagging issues, they are not universally shared. Robert Brain, in his book *Friends and Lovers*, discusses the Bangwa, an African people who very easily achieve strong male-female friendships:

"Bangwa boys and girls form friendships in early childhood and these friendships are never confused with love affairs. They continue throughout the couple's lifetime and do not differ much from informal relations of companionship between men. . . . Moreover, I have since come across other examples in Africa. Among the Nzema of Southern Ghana where friendship is highly valued, formal friendships are instituted between men and women which last their lifetime . . . the two may even sleep together and banish every desire, without any member of the community finding it laughable."

Cease-fire: Platonic Friendships

The Bangwa and other African societies unequivocally demonstrate that platonic friendships are not only possible but can even thrive if the practice is culturally encouraged. This is not to deny "carnal urges" as an element of male-female relationships—our sexual selves are part of our total being—we all have sexual desires, thoughts, fantasies and concerns. Even *Webster's Third New International Dictionary* does not describe platonic relationships as being devoid of any nuance of sex, merely as having the sexual aspect unexpressed. According to the survey respondents, when sex is excluded it is usually because the relationship is built on other facets and either one or both is sexually committed elsewhere—that is, they are married or in love—or because they do not have strong sexual interest in each other. In many such instances, positive experiences are reported.

A forty-two-year-old social worker offered this: "Several years ago, I met a man who has become one of my dearest and closest friends. At least two or three times a month Howard and I spend an evening together. Usually it's sharing a meal, seeing a movie, discussing our work. But the friendship we share is in spirit —it's not in our bodies. Though there are sexual stirrings between us—there always have been and probably always will be—we decided long ago that our relationship would be marred by sexual involvement. We found that we have things to talk about that are different from what he talks about with my husband and different from what I talk about with his wife. There are similar intellectual interests—we always pass on to each other the books that we love—but there's something tender and caring, too. In a couple of instances when I was having a hard time he offered himself, for talking and for helping. And when his father died, he wanted me there—because we care for each other, because we're friends."

A musician, forty-four, overcame an initial sexual setback to develop a rich friendship: "It's only in the past few years that I've made friends with women. There is one woman in particular, Judith, with whom I feel particularly close. When we met a number of years ago, I was a struggling musician whose career was unblemished by any hint of success; I was floundering and basking in self-pity. Judy was a published freelance writer with a bright spirit and a sense of purpose. Our first meeting was at a mutual friend's birthday party and we behaved toward each other on the level of a pornographic soap opera. After all, it was the liberated sixties and sexual freedom was not merely an option—it was a requirement! So much so, that we locked ourselves into a tense drama that night wherein we unenthusiastically ended up in bed together. Needless to say, the sexual experience was a fiasco. Fortunately, we were both good-humored about the whole thing and we were able to see each other not as potential lovers, but as potential friends, good, solid friends. And this is how it has evolved; our relationship is mutually valued but it doesn't encompass sex. It would seem, on the surface, that this is an easy task to accomplish, but in a society that focuses as sharply on the sexual side of life as ours, it was damn hard."

A notable cross-sex friendship was described by a thirty-eight-year-old medical technologist: "Thirteen years ago, when I came to this country from Puerto Rico, I faced several problems simultaneously: adjusting to a new environment, learning the language, meeting new people and earning a living. A year after my arrival here I met David through my job. We are very close, David and I, but ours is not a physical relationship; we are not really attracted to each other in that way. Despite the lack of sexual sparks—or maybe because of it—we've spent many, many hours talking to each other in a very personal way. Over the years, we've come to count on each other's support. With David, I've never felt alone in a foreign land. Three years ago, when I got married, David was as excited and happy for me as were my parents. He has since moved to Colorado but when I was ill last winter, we kept in constant touch by phone. One night he even showed up at the hospital; he flew in just to spend two hours with me. It is no coincidence, now that my husband and I have a son, that we named him David."

The absence of sex, some men and women found, allows for a balanced, honest exchange of feelings that sexual involvement might blur. Free from the jealousies, tensions and restrictions that often surround romantic relationships, barriers are let down, weaknesses are more willingly revealed and intimate confidences are exchanged. A man in his mid-thirties remarked:

"With Ellen, sex may be out of the question, but it is not out of the conversation. She talks to me about the men in her life and I talk to her about my romantic attachments. She has a way of asking the right questions that get me to thinking. It is as if she has an intuitive sensitivity to my inner workings. I feel comfortable talking to her about anything—work, family, half-baked ideas and outrageous fantasies. She never makes me feel like I'm on the spot; I never feel awkward or silly revealing myself to her. With a lover some of these things would just seem too threatening. Being friends with Ellen is special; we know the textures of each other's lives, we are attached to one another yet there is complete freedom in our relationships. We have attachment and commitment without possessiveness, a rare and growth-exchanging combination that I have never achieved in a romance."

And this from a middle-aged woman: "A man once told me he would never have for a friend a woman he would not want to sleep with if he had the opportunity. I can't imagine any woman I know feeling that a prerequisite for friendship with a man would be finding him sexually desirable. Romance is hardly the only road to intimacy. Although many men are interested in women only as love or sex objects, there are men who can be friends with women, who do not base the relationship on sexual attraction. These are men of such excellent character, with such rich personalities, that it would be foolish to pass up the opportunity to know them better. I'd rather have a lasting friendship with somebody like that than a short-term love affair.

"On those rare occasions when I've met a man who is comfortable with his sexuality and secure in his identity, we have had a very valuable friendship that enriched both our lives. One such relationship has survived a number of involvements and dramatic career changes on his part and a marriage, a child and a divorce on my part. He has taught me different things about life and about myself; he has broadened my perspective, added to my insight, challenged me to learn and grow. There has been a greater objectivity between us than usually occurs between lovers. One of the primary virtues of the relationship is that I can say anything to him and he can be completely open with me. That may be a true test of genuine friendship, one that many love affairs would not pass. Sexual/romantic relationships have an obvious excitement and intensity; unfortunately, for me, they also carry with them a pressure to be on my best behavior. With my male friends, I can really let my hair down, I can be completely myself."

While lovers may not always make the best of friends, friendship sometimes survives a misguided fall into bed. Bernice and Allan worked in the same office. Allan found Bernice very attractive. Bernice also found Allan attractive. Bernice was in love with a man who was a trouble-shooting engineer currently on a four-month assignment in South America. She felt she couldn't handle another love relationship, but she did want male companionship. When Allan showed interest, she hesitated and did not want to respond too warmly for fear he would misinterpret her intentions. Finally she agreed to meet him for dinner. Wary, but lonely, Bernice accepted Allan's invitation to return to his apartment after dinner. Not surprisingly, one thing led to another and the relationship threatened to become sexual. Bernice, for her part, reacted to the experience rather dramatically: "When Allan invited me back to his apartment I should have known better, but I felt warmly toward him and took the chance. At first we were having a really good discussion; on the job there really isn't much time to talk and I didn't want to miss out on an opportunity to continue talking with this very interesting guy. He had spent a year traveling all over the world, something I've always wanted to do. He was telling me about the trip, then gradually, he started to touch, to cuddle; in increments he became more sexual. Before long we were about to have intercourse. Suddenly I jumped up and started to run out of the room, crying hysterically. Allan followed me and we had this real blowout. I was confused; I felt duped, naive and deceitful. I felt that I had led him on because of my desperate loneliness—being new in town I really didn't know very many people other than those I met at work. I told Allan that I didn't want to have sex with him even though I liked his company and found him attractive; my love commitment was elsewhere. We agreed to spend time together and have —for the past two years. We are able to laugh about our sexual nightmare and have developed a fine friendship."

The experience also had an impact on Allan: "If I had a heavy investment in proving my masculinity and had taken Bernice's refusal to have sex with me as a putdown, the friendship would never have happened. I can understand Bernice's feelings and I do not ask her to relate to me in a way she doesn't want to. But at the same time, I refuse to castrate myself even now, by pretending that I don't see her as a sexual being. It's really a matter of choice. If I don't press her sexually I receive a valuable friendship. If I pressure with sex, she may defer, but the friendship is sure to go under. It's not worth it."

Just as a friendship sometimes begins in the bedroom, other relationships which ended in the bedroom—love affairs—may resume on a new footing of friendship.

"Carole and I went together for two years. We broke up in anger and didn't see or talk to each other for several months after the separation. One day, she called me and she stated that she missed some of the things we had enjoyed from each other during our love relationship; we both agreed that we were losing something by not being friends. Neither of us had any desire to continue as lovers—we are not sexually involved with one another— but with two years of trust behind us, we can talk about things we don't discuss with anyone else. It's great."

It seems to be an idealized image: a relationship of lovers moving from passion and romance through the agony of separation only to be reborn into fulfilling friends. In actuality, it is a rare experience that only a small minority of individuals questioned had achieved. For many people—particularly the insecure —hidden feelings of proprietorship interfere with the development of friendship. Being used to the intensity of passion and romance in a love relationship makes it very difficult to shift gears, to give up expectations and settle for what in many people's view is a lesser relationship. Nonetheless, as is often true in human ationships, the effort to surmount the difficulty has rich rewards. The trust and love built over a long period of interacting can provide a fertile soil for a solid friendship.

Exception to the Sexual Rule: Pillow Pals

Some men and women may start out as friends, have a sexual relationship for a while, then end up "just" friends again; others, former lovers, may renew their relationship as platonic friendship; in still other instances it can and does happen that a sexual relationship coexists with friendship although the participants do not consider themselves lovers. Can this really be considered friendship rather than a love affair? The first step in answering this question would be to define both love and friendship with exactitude—a task on which many scholars and philosophers have labored without success. Friends, like lovers, admire each other; lovers, like friends, do things for each other; friends and lovers both show concern, communicate using special words, share private jokes and so on. Despite all existing knowledge, the meaning of, or distinction between friendship and love relations is still subject to personal opinion. For this reason, discriminating between the two was left to each respondent's discretion.

Patrick, a forty-six-year-old sculptor, looks placid, content and uncomplicated. His features are sharp and clear. His hair is graying, giving him a distinctive appearance which clashes with his casual, sometimes careless manner of dress. Although Patrick is an accomplished artist, he has few friends in his field. Due partially to a basic shyness and to overwork, he rarely socializes. More important, he feels himself to be an outsider in the arts. Unlike his colleagues, whom he views as freewheeling and liberal, Patrick's tastes and many of his convictions stem from a conservative, stoic base. Raised in a comfortable Irish-Catholic home in a small, closely knit community, he is considered even there as something of an oddity: "What's a Harvard-educated man doing with a chisel, chipping away at stone?" Patrick, too, sometimes feels he should have been a scientist, an engineer, something of substance. Loved by his family, but not accepted, respected by his peers, but not understood, Patrick has spent most of his adult life alone, consoled only by his prodigious outpouring of art. Far from placid, content and uncomplicated, as appearances would indicate, this is a restless, complex man who has alienated himself from his own feelings. Several years ago, though, on a trip to Boston promoting his work, he happened upon a woman who added a glow to his life. His eyes sparkled as he talked about the relationship:

"Strange how it happened. I was making one of those dreaded but necessary personal appearances at a showing of my work, and instead of heading straight back to my hotel as is my habit, that evening I took a walk and wandered into a crowded bar. At first I was repelled by the crowd, but again I relented from my usual avoidance of people and allowed myself to feel the warmth and comfort of the human flesh surrounding me. I squeezed my way to an unused cubicle of space and sat facing the back of a young woman. Later in the evening her female companion left and she turned in my direction. From the moment we sat facing each other, speechless at first, it felt good to me. It felt right. We drank and we talked, and talked and drank, until we were both very high and had told each other an awful lot about ourselves. We returned to my hotel early that morning and made love. And then lying side by side, we talked some more and made love again. We discussed the books we were reading, movies we had seen, my hopes and artistic aspirations, her work. We talked about our childhoods, our growing up, we talked ourselves to sleep.

"The next day, sobered, we both went off in different directions, I to my last appearance, she to a writing assignment. We agreed to meet for dinner. This was no small task, just breaking my usual one-hundred-percent business and efficiency routine was monumental for me. After all, I was due back home in California. I had work waiting for me. But she was so irresistibly refreshing. She was small and slender, almost childlike, with black, shiny hair. When she spoke, she looked even prettier. There was something about her warmth and personality that attracted me. We continued our conversation right where we had left off and talked all the way through dinner and into the late evening. Then we had sex again. It was fantastic. I had never been as sexually excited as I was with her. But this wasn't the important thing; most important to me was the way I felt about myself when I was with her. This is when I first became aware of how distant I am from my feelings. In the weeks and months that followed, we saw each other several times—either I flew to Boston or we met for a weekend elsewhere—and she confronted me gently but constantly. In a compassionate and caring way, she prodded me to express my feelings, to act on them, to be alive! We did such outrageous things together. I felt less controlled. I was trusting myself more, trusting my instincts. My work took on new, less constrained dimensions."

Patrick does not consider Janet, the woman he met in Boston, to be his lover. He continues to be mostly a loner, still travels to see Janet on occasion—four years after their first meeting—but is too absorbed in his career, as she is in hers, for a serious love affair. The two see each other when they can, and aside from sex, take an interest in each other's work, share enjoyment of food, music, nature, art and movies. Other than that, their lives don't intersect on a regular basis much, because of the distance between them and their mutual dedication to demanding careers. Asked to comment on the relationship, Janet wrote the following:

"Patrick and I are friends, not lovers. Our relationship is the ideal compromise between the excesses of romantic passion and the guilt-producing disconnectedness of impersonal sex. Over the years, I have had several such friendships with men. The quality and extent of the sexual interest has varied greatly; it has been marginal and unimportant as well as constituting the primary basis for the friendship. I have found that sex, rather than inter-fering, can be a positive element in a friendship. I say this know-ing that there is not necessarily a hard-and-fast line that can be drawn between sexual friendship and romantic love; sex is now more readily available to men and women, and the line between friendship and love affairs is less distinct.

"Yet, whatever love or friendship may be in a philosophic sense, they are not identical; lovers need not be equals, though unequals can rarely be friends. Patrick and I regard each other as equals; lovers are more absorbed in their feelings about each other than ideas or interests outside themselves. Patrick and I delight in our mutual interests; love affairs can thrive despite little communication, friendship depends upon interaction. The more things Patrick and I do together or say to each other, the closer we feel. While lovers place total importance on romance and sex, Patrick and I might see each other several times without sex. Then, we get together, our eyes meet and there's a sexual spark. There is a fluidity here, for whatever does or does not happen sexually, it is no threat to our bond. It's very simple; we help each other through the night and in the morning leave each other free to go about our own business. Sex is a bonus to our camaraderie."

Issues and Answers

Close opposite-sex friendships were reported by eighteen percent—less than two out of ten—of our survey respondents. This is a striking finding which does not speak well for the relations between the sexes. In point of fact, male-female ties—not bound by lover status or marriage—are rare and precarious; neither men nor women, for the most part, find them comfortable or easy to establish. Some forty percent, either disinterested or discouraged, do not even express a desire for such friendship. It is difficult to give up myths and old securities, to work out ways of relating that surmount sexual and sexist issues—the most common friendship complaints that men and women direct toward one another. Yet, those who do this—who know their differences do not make them inferior or superior and who can balance their eroticism with the demands of friendship—find that opposite-sex relationships add immeasurably to their existence.

Opportunities to form cross-sex friendships, particularly for women, are enhanced by employment (a good mix of males and females in relatively noncompetitive positions, as is sometimes found in education and health-related professions, is ideal) and by membership in professional, voluntary and recreational associations. As with same-sex friendships, men and women choose opposite-sex friends who are reasonably similar in age and education. It seems that in most friendships, birds of similar background flock together. When homogeneity does not prevail, the men frequently were older and better educated than their female friends, features placing the man in the superordinate position. Interestingly, this variation on the part of both males and females parallels the differences found in courtship and marriage.

The presence of sexual attraction in a friendship invites a formidable quandary. Not surprisingly, this issue is escalated when one or both friends are married. Although most concede that they cannot be all things to each other, fulfill all of one another's needs, a bondage of marriage often requires that they restrict their contact with others, especially those of the opposite sex. Only six out of one hundred married respondents report having an opposite-sex friend. In interviews pursuing this question, uneasiness was often in the air, suspicion was the dominant theme; an ample supply of justification was proffered: "I wouldn't trust him [her]"; "too tempting"; "looking for trouble"; "bound to evolve into something sexual"; "won't work." Even many couples who describe themselves as liberal were restrictive and cautious in this regard. "You can have lunch with him," one man told his wife, "but seeing him after work for any reason makes me very uncomfortable."

Perhaps due to greater opportunity and desire as well as to the absence of stumbling blocks—such as possessiveness and jealousy —found in many marital relationships, single individuals account for the majority of male-female friendships. Even among singles, though, these friendships are described as more difficult to develop than friendships with members of the same sex. Additionally (with some exceptions), the friendships they do describe are not spoken of with the fervor reserved for love relationships. In this sense, the majority of individuals interviewed regarded friendship as something less than love; its consequences are far less sought after. Consistency is not one of the most dominant of human characteristics; although many singles talked of the value of platonic friendships, they also stated they had little time for them because they were busy dating and were seeking a romantic alliance. "Friendship with a man," observed a young woman, "no matter how great the dedication and how lively the contact, leaves dead spaces when compared to romantic attachments."

If a male-female relationship moves from the platonic to the sexual, conflict is likely to compete with friendship feelings. Again, this need not be, but most people queried found that if sex can be switched on or off as the situation demands, "off" is the position that favors a more lasting friendship. In the psychology of close relationships, as in everything else, there are individual differences which affect outcome; some people are better suited than others by temperament and outlook to be successful at forming sexual friendships. People who are better prepared do not attach great emotional weight to sex, do not have a desperate sexual neediness and are able to enjoy other people sexually from time to time without demands of exclusivity. Even here, a very strong friendship bond is required so that the inclusion of sex does not dilute the relationship's value.

For those people whose emotional makeup is more intense, the lack of commitment—having sex and maintaining a close attachment with someone who isn't "yours"—is likely to be sheer torture. Far from being a panacea, for most of us in this society, with our emotional equipment, balancing occasional sex with the intensity of close friendship produces conflict and jealousy. Obviously, any given solution to this dilemma will prove useful to some and destructive to others. The advocacy of a single prescription is useless: What may apply to one person will not apply to another; and what is true for one person at a particular period in life, may not be true for that same person at a later period. Over the centuries, we have been offered numerous formulas for opposite-sex friendships by self-proclaimed saviors, revolutionaries, prophets, behavioral scientists and philosophers, and not one of them has proved ideal for all. Ideal solutions exist only in an ideal world; in the real world, the best we can do is to seek options that fit our individual natures and do not violate our cherished values.

Marriage and Friendship:
The Lonely Crowd

Strangers in the Night, and in the Daytime, Too

MARRIAGE IS, among other things, a friendship agreement. If it is not a friendship—that is, if it is not companionable—then it will probably prove to be an unsatisfactory human relationship. Of all the ties holding couples together—shared parenting roles, finances, a home and property—marriage is likely to succeed in proportion to the degree of companionship it provides. And, in fact, with divorce being elected by more than one family in three, friendship in marriage is a goal accomplished by too few of us. Even with romantic feelings, compatible sexuality and a successful division of family responsibilities, a marriage lacking in companionship may still leave a man or woman frustrated and empty.

"Our meeting was absolutely beautiful and very romantic. Joseph was a blind date arranged through a mutual friend. I don't

109

ordinarily make blind dates, but my friend really urged me on this one. She was right! We went to dinner but never noticed the food. We couldn't talk enough, we got misty-eyed again and again; we were so enraptured with each other. Joseph and I went back to his apartment and we talked and made love almost all night. I had had plenty of relationships that were mostly sexual but I knew this one was different, and so did Joseph. After three months, when he asked me to marry him, I wasn't surprised—it was natural and inevitable.

"The beginning of our marriage continued in the direction of our courtship; we both shared a sense of warmth, a feeling of being loved, a feeling of having taken out an option on a partnership. We considered ourselves to be best friends. Talking together made us feel very close. We told things to each other that we'd never confided to anyone else. Sometimes we'd lie in bed and talk into the small hours of morning. The whole world seemed to spread out for us to explore together. But as open and emotional as we were in those early days of our relationship, just so shut and frozen did we become over the years. Now we have so little to say. Little by little we have bottled up our feelings—both of love and of resentment—until we seem to feel nothing at all for each other.

"The friendship seems to have gone out of our marriage. Our sense of each other, the companionship had been superb when we just met; over the years it faded and shrank until our original ecstasy was no longer recognizable. We were simply too busy— he with his career, I with the responsibilities of our home and family—to notice that we were no longer friends. The signals were there but we just refused to recognize them. He would retreat as soon as he came home, to the garage where he worked on restoring an antique car, or into the den where he built ship models. On those occasions when he was receptive or cheerful, I was resentful of all the times he wasn't and, spitefully, did not make myself available. In return, when I took an initiative to talk, he would demonstrate his disinterest by promptly falling asleep. After a while, conversation just about dried up; there is nearly a total lack of communication between us on philosophies of life, goals, personal dreams, etc. The only topics we discuss are the weather, the children's clothing and the price of food at the supermarket.

"The ironic thing about this is that my friends who knew us when we were enthusiastic about our relationship would always rib us about our nonstop talking. They would comment that going out with us felt like an intrusion—we were so taken by our own conversation that they hated to interrupt. That seems like a very long time ago; now we are together for the simple reason that we cannot endure the thought of living alone. I have cultivated a kind of existential resignation and wry humor about the whole thing: 'Don't take it all so hard,' I tell myself, 'all marriages are like this!' But in all honesty, I don't really believe that. There must be more to it. All the women's magazines from *Redbook* to *Cosmopolitan* always give the same advice: Stroke him, massage his ego, tell him what he wants to hear, pretend. That's such a bunch of nonsense. How can I have a 'repair' conversation based on dishonesty and deceit. It is difficult enough to be agonized by the void in our relationship. I am not about to add lies and deception to our comedy of errors. The problem is, at this stage of our relationship, how can I express my true feelings and needs in such a way that is not threatening or seen as blaming. Lately, I have felt that the real barrier between us—the cause of our lost friendship—is not really the inability to talk, but the lack of empathy between us. We have become strangers to each other's experience of life."

People marry dreaming of love—the romantic and erotic components in a relationship. Nonetheless, a large part of the daily emotional nourishment in marriage springs not from romance but from friendship. Performing whatever duties are called for in a marriage—provider, parent, sex partner—is enough to make the relationship functional. It is not enough to assure satisfaction. For that, companionship must be added to the marital stew. When asked to choose the most important aspect of marriage—sexual satisfaction, companionship (friendship), material things (accumulation of possessions), the opportunity to have children, someone to turn to for problem solving—companionship was way out in front as the first choice by both husbands and wives participating in the survey.

Other investigations are corroborative of these findings. In a host of studies involving several hundred couples, companionship was ranked highest. Sexual adjustment, as in our survey, ran, at best, a distant second to companionship. One man, explaining why his marriage did not last, illustrates the relatively greater weight assigned to companionship as contrasted to sexuality:

"Doris and I had at least two essentials that seem important for a good marriage: We respected each other and we were attracted to each other sexually. That, according to many people (particularly our parents) should have been enough. But it wasn't; there was a large, hollow gulf in between our sexual contacts. There was only a minimum of talk and what there was, more often than not, involved the business of marriage: 'Did you pick up milk; who's driving Kevin to soccer; did anyone call?' We didn't fight a lot or even disagree much. That wasn't the problem. There was no fun in our relationship; none of that delightful intimacy and joyfulness that is associated with a close friendship. And, no matter what the marriage experts say, neither respect nor good sex nor both combined is enough. If I marry again it is companionship that I will be seeking. The rest will fall into place. There is a woman in my life now. Her figure is not as sexy as Doris's, but I have a great time with her; we can talk intimately and we are interested in each other. That is what I need."

Talk to Me!

If companionship is so highly valued in marriage, the corresponding issue arises: How is it achieved? This matter was pursued at length in many of the follow-up interviews. Here, men and women fell out of agreement. While many women prescribed good communication as an overall panacea for companionship, men were not as enthusiastic or as hopeful that this was the key to marital friendship. Men were, however, unable to offer a counterproposal. Thus, while husbands and wives attach similar values to companionship in marriage, women have a more definitive view of how the task is to be accomplished. Men, on the whole, are skeptical and probably a bit uneasy with their wives' admonishment: Talk to me!

And, herein lies a major conflict in marital life. Enduring friendship requires that individuals supply one another with a great deal of pertinent information. In many marriages though, an opposite process, one of noncommunication, occurs. (What he doesn't know won't hurt him. The best thing may be not to tell her. Why bother my wife with professional or business issues she really doesn't understand? Why trouble my husband with the children's misbehavior? He has enough to worry about.) It is not surprising that many letters to the advice-giving sages in the daily press deal with problems of this kind. There is an impressive research literature documenting the association of good communication between spouses and satisfying marriages. It shows rather conclusively that openness of communication is an excellent source of marital friendship.

Despite its proven value, one reason open marital communication is so hard to come by is that the companionable marriage is a relatively new phenomenon, and very little in our education has prepared us for it. It is difficult to imagine how revolutionary the idea is that husband and wives should be friends with one another. Men and women have always been sexually attracted to each other, and there is an enormous literature on sexual relations between spouses. But there is only very recently an emphasis on good social relations between the sexes in marriage. Most middle-aged adults today grew up in a household in which friendship between their parents was not even considered an aspired goal. Against the plea for openness between husband and wife are pitted the long-standing social facts of life: "If you talk too much you give yourself away; you give her (him) something to use against you." Deceptions and lies are almost institutionalized, standard operating procedures between the sexes. As a result, rather than sharing the closeness of a friendship, many husbands and wives live in their very separate emotional worlds.

A lifetime of inattentiveness to feelings, discussed in my book, *The Other Man, The Other Woman,* is strikingly demonstrated by Martin, a musician, and Gloria, his wife of twenty years. Two months before this conversation, Gloria had discovered Martin's long-standing infidelity:

> Martin: I don't think we've even been a team intimately. I've never felt close to you. I've always felt you were my doll. You were my gracious hostess, my lovely lady, my bride. I loved you with reservation. As though you were a piece of art and would surely break if I were to release my passion on you and in you. So, throughout the years, I've sought to release this passion with other women.
>
> Therapist: Gloria, how did you feel about the relationship all these years?
>
> Gloria: How did I feel? Well . . . I suppose lonely. I wanted to be with Martin more. I wanted to be more passionate with him, less reserved, but I always felt he would reject me. I always felt he wanted me up on a pedestal. I stayed there to keep him.
>
> Martin: (Stunned) But, Gloria, I never knew that. Why didn't you tell me how you felt? Why didn't you say something?
>
> Gloria: Afraid, I guess. You never asked. I thought that was the way you wanted things.
>
> Therapist: Martin, how come you never said anything?
>
> Martin: (Crying) For the same reason, I suppose. I took it for granted that Gloria was happy with the status quo. I didn't want to hurt her or be hurt. God, I wish I had known how you felt back then, Gloria. I didn't really want to see other women. I wanted intimacy. Closeness. We could have given that to each other.

The waste of time, energy and potential friendship through the years of Martin and Gloria's marriage, when what they both *really* wanted was so much more similar than what they each *supposed* the other wanted, is appalling. Yet, this same kind of waste was alluded to by many of our respondents and probably affects millions of marriages. Survey responses disclose that a mere thirty-eight percent of married persons consider their spouses to have the qualities of a good friend. One of the most thought-provoking results of the considerable research efforts in this area is how little husbands and wives really do know or understand one another. "I know him (her) like the back of my hand," brags a husband or wife. Yet, under experimental conditions, their performance more closely resembles the comical, embarrassingly inaccurate mates of the "Newlywed Game" than teammates who correctly assess each other's signals.

Even in the simplest kind of predictions of one another's behavior, couples are usually wrong. In a report published in *Marriage and Family Living*, researchers asked spouses which one of them would tend to talk more during a decision-making process dealing with how they would spend a hypothetical gift of several hundred dollars. The session was recorded so that the actual amount of talking done by each could be measured. Only seventeen out of fifty individuals correctly calculated who would be the more active negotiator. What's more, after the session was over and the participants were again asked who had talked more, over half still judged incorrectly!

In another study, investigators increased the participants' motivation to forecast correctly by presenting actual rewards for success. Husbands and wives in separate rooms were shown an assortment of items—gloves, scarves, belts, lingerie, wallets— some suitable for men, some for women. If, without communication, they could successfully coordinate their choices—that is, choose the same item—they would receive the items as rewards. They all failed. Not one of the twenty-five couples participating succeeded in predicting one another's choices on as many as five of the twenty items.

In still another study, this time involving 116 couples, each partner was asked separately to give the names of persons considered by both spouses to be close mutual friends, not counting relatives. In an astonishing result, only 6 couples were in total accord on this task, while one couple were in complete disagreement regarding their mutual friends.

Not surprisingly, couples who have a solid, companionable relationship understand each other better than those who are unhappily married. One study of eighty-two such couples and eighty unsatisfactorily married spouses revealed that nearly three-quarters of the former but less than half of the latter couples agreed in their checking of an elaborate 128-item questionnaire concerned with their perception of themselves and of their spouses. It may be, of course, that husbands and wives have a good understanding of each other because the marital relationship is friendship-oriented to begin with, or they may achieve a friendship-type relationship because they have a good understanding of each other, or both. Whatever the direction of the association, however, a major feature in marriages lacking in friendship is the failure of husbands and wives to be attuned to each other's feelings.

There may be any number of reasons for this plight: If reared in a uncommunicative family, an individual may not have developed adequate verbal skills. Some people are shy; they may lack self-confidence ("Why should anyone want to listen to me? I have nothing important to say."). Some become intimidated, while others are hostile and do not communicate in order not to antagonize. Still others are suspicious, self-protective and hence secretive. One thing is certain: To understand another person's thoughts and feelings, thoroughly, and to be thoroughly understood by this other person in return—this is one of the most rewarding of human experiences and, unfortunately, all too rare in marriage.

Belle Indifférence: The Middle Years of Marital Friendship

As is true of all long-term relationships, husband-wife friendships vary along the dimensions of time. Most people think that marriage is at first made up of discovery, of having novel emotions and impressions, of conflict, and of finding new ways of sharing, all of which slowly evolves into a more stable but ever more complete and satisfying friendship. According to the majority of interviewed couples who were married long enough to have a perspective on this issue, however, the actual curve of marital friendship is more complex. When the fire of romance is banked and as passion cools, the marriage frequently becomes boring and stale. For a good many years, there is often a period of decline rather than increased companionship. During this long stretch— a time when daily pressures and responsibilities are greatest— words like monotony, humdrum and fed up describe the state of many marriages.

Predictably, most husbands and wives reported the kind of relationship in their early married years that typifies close friends —the exploring and mutual discussion of beliefs, inner feelings, likes and dislikes, comparing of ideas and plans for the future. But as the relationship grew more complex with the coming of children, the acquisition of a home, more time-consuming duties and increased career involvement, the amount of companionship and the intensity of satisfaction it yielded diminished dramatically. In striking contrast to the enthusiasm of courtship, conversation became painfully strained. For instance:

She: You never talk to me.
He: What's on your mind?
She: It's not what's on my mind, it's that I never know what's on your mind.
He: What do you want to know?
She: Everything!
He: That's ridiculous.
She: (Angry) I'll bet you don't think talking to that blonde assistant of yours is ridiculous!

He: Aw, come on, cut it out.

She: (On the verge of tears) You never want to talk to me any more the way you did when we were going together.

He: Here we go again.

Of all the additions of married life that cut into husband-wife companionship, the impact of children hits hardest. Parents of preschoolers were about three times less likely to consider their spouses as friends than were childless couples or parents of older children. Being a parent, as Sigmund Freud once remarked, is an impossible profession even under the best of circumstances. When three generations of family members lived in the same house or nearby, it was easier to raise children. Grandparents and aunts could take over a while so that a couple could have some time to themselves; today's parents carry the responsibility for being everything to their children. And usually, it is an unequal division of labor; the woman becomes housebound and child-occupied while her husband becomes money and career-oriented. A gap steadily widens between their life experiences, funds of information and interests. With the coming of children the exchange of the friendship they savored is transformed into an occasional grunt or less.

Marcia and Norman have been married for four years. For the first three years of their marriage, they both worked—Norman as a pharmacist, Marcia as a teacher. During those three years, Norman and Marcia shared a common goal—purchasing a home —which they accomplished. At the end of their third year of marriage, two things happened: Marcia gave birth and Norman opened his own pharmacy. As a result of these events, Norman and Marcia experienced a dramatic change in their usual routine. Marcia left her teaching position and was at home all day caring for the child. Norman was home less because of his increased responsibility. When Norman returned home, he was sometimes irritable and usually quite fatigued. Often, he was greeted by a wife who felt equally off color. To prepare himself for the unpleasant news and growing friction at home, Norman began to stop for a drink after work. Marcia, disgusted with the unpredictability of his arrival home, stopped preparing meals. Norman, in turn, began eating out more frequently. They became more and more distant:

Norman: It used to be that we sat down, had cocktails and a leisurely meal together. We would discuss our day and enjoy each other's company. Then I came home and the house was a mess, the meal was lousy and I was greeted by a tiger ready to lunge at me.

Marcia: I felt Norman no longer had any interest in me. He seemed to have more interest in his business. When he came home, all he wanted to do was eat quickly, watch TV and go to sleep. When I suggested that we go out together after the baby went to sleep, he constantly refused because he was tired. Well, I was tired also, but I desperately needed his companionship.

Norman: We seemed to have been unprepared for the extreme change in our lives. Our son added fulfillment to our lives, but he also exacted a price.

A price indeed. A large-scale research effort conducted through Cornell University revealed that the average parents of preschool children talk to each other only about half as much per day as they did in the intimacy of their first years of marriage. This in itself is not necessarily corrosive; the dwindling quantity is minor compared to the painful change of quality. Researchers found conversations once spiced with exchanges about books, ideas and personal relationships were almost entirely concerned with routine affairs—"What did you do today, dear?" . . . "Oh, nothing much. . . . What did you do?" . . . "Was there anything in the mail?" . . . "The plumber came to fix the sink." In effect, husbands and wives were using the mundane words of business partners rather than the emotionally and intellectually richer ones of friends. This experience was common to many of our survey respondents. "On one occasion," the mother of two preschoolers wrote, "we went to Marriage Encounter and we were told to forget we were married and get to know each other as two human beings. That was a terrific idea, we stayed up half the night talking to each other. Unfortunately, when we returned home, we eventually fell into the same pattern of disinterest."

For some husbands and wives, the gap developed during the early parenting years becomes too wide and the companionship lost is never regained; there is a lack of both the motivation and the skill necessary to reconstruct the original connection. Frequently, as many of my respondents found, their aloneness with each other surfaces somewhere between eight and ten years of marriage. This corresponds to the period when the divorce rates are very high; it is a time when the parenting function is not quite as consuming, the career is launched and revaluation of the relationship comes into consideration. If it is a time when many people join the ranks of the formerly married, this occurs not so much because the passion left the union but, more crucially, because they no longer feel they have anything in common, little to be friends about and, consequently, no reason to remain married. One man, deeply tanned and prosperous-looking, who had been married ten years, explained:

"We were sitting in an exclusive seaside restaurant one night having dinner. As on many other nights, we were aware of each other but only vaguely. This night my attention was directed on a younger couple seated nearby—a man and women locked in each other's gaze, speaking softly, inaudibly, sometimes laughing together, other times looking very serious, playful and earnest, all the while holding hands. I thought to myself: 'We were like that. What happened? How did the bottom fall out?' I realized that my feelings of being disconnected from Rebecca had been bugging me for some time. When we talked about this it became evident we were already divorced, we were practicing an invisible divorce. Yes, we lived under one roof, slept in the same bed, but we had withdrawn from each other long ago. I contacted a lawyer after that and began to formalize the breakup."

Of course, the strain of preschool children on marriage does not always contribute to the dissolution of the relationship, nor does it necessarily have to weaken it; with the burden of parenthood comes a supply of equivalent or even greater joys. However, the companionship aspect of the marital relationship almost always suffers. As numerous parents of young children who continued to have an active (but dormant) interest in each other and who were still desirous of one another's companionship testified, it is an uphill battle to obtain the time in which to be companionable. Some couples may feed the children early so that they may have a late dinner alone; others may make a purposeful decision to cram one or two evenings with household duties so that the remaining nights afford relaxation and time together. Still others plan to go out to dinner regularly, leaving children, phone, dog and responsibilities behind. Though these strategies are useful, they are far from perfect—fatigue, interminable childhood demands and the limits of emotional resources may foul the best attempts at privacy—and the disagreeable fact remains that until children are of school age, marital friendship often sinks into remission.

And then, as the children grow more self-sufficient—usually in the second decade of marriage—for some couples marital friendship is renewed; like a blossoming plant it shines with life and fresh color. With more time for each other the conversation may return to shared experiences, cultural topics, discussions of friends. Listen to one woman with two children aged eight and ten who, two years ago, began to work part-time:

"When the children were small Harold and I were in separate worlds. I had my tales of woe concerning the misdeeds of one of the children and he had a triumph to tell from his day's activities. We both listened dutifully and pretended to be very interested, but we were bored and didn't really appreciate what the other was talking about. Neither of us was fooled by what was happening and after a while conversation decreased sharply. Now that we have more time and are less hemmed-in than in the past, we are more tolerant listeners and we have things of value to say in return. Our lives are less pressured and consequently we are more able to be sympathetic to each other's triumphs and failures. It's beautiful. We go out together, do many things jointly, talk more; we have the time to understand each other. We're involved, our marriage is companionable again. It's like we both renewed a long-lost friendship."

The Growth of Marital Friendship

What accounts for the difference? Why is there a recovery of companionship in some marriages and not in others? Aside from personality factors which enter into any complex human interaction, the most common answer has been that couples who are not companionable when time allows were probably never really companionable. These marriages, it is reasoned, were formed primarily on temporary infatuation and had no true basis for closeness. Undeniably, some people's choice of a mate rests on ready availability rather than sound judgment. They may think themselves in the grip of a special and unduplicated passion but, out of insecurity, neurotic deprivation or overwhelming pressure from family and friends, they choose unwisely. Yet, this is not always the case. In discussion with hundreds of the formerly married for my book *To Marry Again*, it was evident that many couples who were initially well matched become unmatched with the passage to time due to major differences in their personal growth and development.

A particularly common aspect of this unmatching process was described, as noted earlier, most frequently by couples operating within the framework of what might be described as a "traditional" marriage: She takes primary responsibility for the children, prepares meals and cleans the house. He provides the income, makes household repairs and is second in command with the children on weekends. By the assignment of career exclusively to the husband and homemaking exclusively to the wife, the disparity of intellectual worldliness between the couple is likely to deepen and, consequently, the basis for marital friendship is severely narrowed.

In contrast to this pitfall (and occasionally despite it), some individuals manage to grow along with each other. These are the couples who stand a far better chance of renewing and intensifying their marital friendship. In this regard, the following trends were observed among survey respondents: Wives who work (even part-time) more often considered their husbands to be a friend than did homemakers. Women who are college students were similarly more likely to report their marriage as having friendship qualities. Interviews revealed that college women were more likely than women of equal economic status but less education to develop outside interests—probably as with employed activity, outside interests help bridge the "mental stimulation/things in common" gap. Men who were favorable to the Women's Movement (and presumably encouraged their wives' personal growth) reported a more frequent incidence of marital friendship than those men who react unfavorably to this issue.

Consider the views of Kenneth, a highly respected, award-winning photographer and the father of three children. He is a man who is occasionally exasperated by his wife but most often delighted and pleased by her company. "She is," he stated at the outset of our conversation, "my very best friend."

"I first met Nancy one summer weekend on the beach. It was an overcast day and the beach was nearly empty. I was just about to return home when I spotted this tall, good-looking redhead sitting alone. When I approached her she looked up matter-of-factly from her book—*Elements of Embryology*, of all things—and wasn't particularly friendly. But I was gently persistent. She told me, finally, that she was completing her doctorate in biology. I was pretty impressed; she really had exciting, ambitious goals. Finding a guy and getting married wasn't a top priority as it was with lots of women I encountered. What struck me about her was that she was so alive, so interesting. After we had relaxed a bit we seemed to have so much to talk about. This wasn't just a beautiful woman; there was a real person under that pretty skin.

"We continued to see each other and the following year Nancy graduated and accepted a very prestigious postdoctoral research position at Harvard. For the first couple of months I commuted to Boston and we spent our weekends together. After a while, though, we realized how much we missed each other's company during the week. I moved my stuff up to Boston—as a pretty well established freelance, moving was no problem—and we found a little place. I'd come back home after a day's work, we'd go out for a quick dinner and then return home where I'd help her study until late at night. It was a grind, but I really loved seeing her progress, she has such a fine mix of the scientific, the philosophical and the artistic mind. I felt about her as I had never felt about anyone. I was proud to know her.

"We were married that fall and over the next eight years our three daughters—Jennifer, Katharine and Alyson—were born. Nancy is still enormously involved in science, she has a university faculty position, she is active in professional organizations and she is a frequent contributor to the professional literature. I, as usual, am passionately devoted to my work. Our life is busy, hectic, frequently bordering on the chaotic. I guess it's always been this way—even before the children. There have been periods when for days at a time we meet each other only in bed. And nowadays, with the kids, especially if someone gets sick, the confusion at times is barely tolerable. I know Nancy is concerned about the impact of her frequent absence on the children; I often worry about my time with them also. But when I really stop to think about it, they're getting along beautifully. They are thriving psychologically.

"There are times when I think it would be much simpler, easier, more harmonious if Nancy didn't work, if she was more of a housewife. I think of my parents—my father worked and my mother catered to him. Life revolved around him. Honestly, sometimes when I'm dealing with the girls and I'm hungry and tired,

I wish my wife was a bit more domesticated. But then Nancy and I go out together and I see other couples looking bored with each other, hardly ever making eye contact, not having anything to say to each other. That's when I reaffirm what we've developed. We're *still* courting each other—after sixteen years. We always find each other interesting, stimulating. When Nancy talks about her work her excitement is infectious. I don't know if I would be as pleased if I wasn't pretty successful in my own field, but I am. She has great respect for my own work and that means a lot to me. All in all, even though life with us is never simple, and sometimes things can even be very rough, there is no one I'd rather spend an evening with than Nancy."

No doubt, the way of life described above is busy and complicated; it calls for the scheduling talent of a network executive, the flexibility of a labor-relations negotiator and the energy of a politician campaigning for reelection. Yet, although it may not be every couple's solution, it does provide this man and woman the mutual growth necessary for continued friendship. And this is the task before each couple: to discover for themselves workable ways to keep the marital friendship alive. However the task is achieved, whatever methods are used, it is evident that marital friendship, as with friendship generally, does not flourish automatically. Quite to the contrary, it requires considerable thought, sensitivity and hard work.

Widening Horizons

Most of us know that even at its best marriage cannot meet all the needs of both spouses all the time. Previous to marriage, friends play a part in meeting these needs. After marriage, the way in which friendships are played out and the place they have in our lives shift. The focus of friendship often moves from a regularly nurtured relationship to a once-in-a-while get-together when the concerns of marriage, children, relatives and work can be put aside. As we have seen, opposite-sex friends suffer dramatically. In these instances it is not usually time or other priorities that interfere, it is the nagging question: But what if the satisfaction threatens to become sexual? This is the eventuality that many of the married fear. As a result, premarital opposite-sex friendships are frequently dropped and new ones, if not actually discouraged, are a continuing source of conflict. Recall, only six percent of married individuals acknowledged an opposite-sex friend.

The contention between one couple, Tony and Roberta, illustrates a common occurrence. For the first eight years of their marriage, both busied themselves with the usual responsibilities of husband and wife: Tony earned a comfortable living as an attorney. Roberta ran the house and was primarily responsible for the children. With both children in school, Roberta felt the need for stimulation outside her role as homemaker and joined a community photography workshop. Not only did she enjoy photography, but as a stranger in the group she was pleasantly surprised to find that the instructor was an old friend of hers from college. She and Harold, who was now divorced, very much enjoyed talking over old times. After a few weeks, however, it became clear that Tony was jealous, and he insisted that she quit the photography workshop. "After all," he declared, "I avoid friendships with women." The fact that Roberta didn't quietly comply only served to raise Tony's suspicions. Eventually, as the strain surrounding this conflict increased, Roberta gave up her renewed friendship "for the sake of the marriage."

In effect, even though practically all of us have desires for a wide range of interpersonal relationships and for a variety of people outside the marital relationship, when it comes to anything resembling a potential challenge from the opposite sex, possessiveness is still very much in vogue. A serious drawback of this posture is the missed opportunity to gain further understanding of the opposite sex and thus of one's own mate. If a wife can have only female friends, the husband only male friends, both are prevented from knowing one another more fully as individual people sharing a common humanity. Roberta, by being restricted to female friends, becomes more involuted into femaleness; Tony, by allowing himself male friendships exclusively, emphasizes those aspects of his being which he shares only with other males. Each grows further away from understanding the other; both become further entrenched in their male or female separations. Ironically, this position, designed to protect the marriage from opposite-sex "intruders," more often results in a prison of boredom and frustration from which, as time passes, escape is sought.

In a chance meeting two years after the initial interview, Roberta had this to say: "Things went from uncomfortable to smothering. When we went out socially, Tony clung to me as if we were chained to one another. One night in particular we had a terrible blowup. We were at a party and Tony went into the kitchen—only because his friend wanted to talk with him. When he returned, I was on the sofa in the living room talking intently to a man Tony didn't know. He rushed over to join us and when I introduced him he was perfectly polite. But then he kept disputing everything this man said and was very argumentative and obnoxious. It was clear that he was conveying the message: 'She's mine. Get away from her, you're not wanted here.' And indeed, this man took the hint and excused himself. I was utterly embarrassed and humiliated.

"On another occasion when Tony was working late, my friend Diane called to suggest that I join her and her fiancé, Roger, for a drink after work. Since Tony was going to be late anyway, I agreed. I had such a good time with Diane and Roger that when I noticed the time it was later than I realized. I called Tony to tell him why I wasn't home. He had been home only a few minutes himself but he was furious. He accused me of seeing another man and demanded I put Diane on the phone. This time I didn't concede and simply slammed down the receiver. At first my resentments toward Tony for his restrictions and interferences with my friendships were small and minor. But as my frustration mounted, as his nagging and suspicion increased, it became intolerable. Last year I insisted that we go for marriage counseling. He refused, saying that there was nothing wrong. That did it. I left."

Tony's jealousy was obviously extreme—for the majority of couples things do not work out so drastically. However, judging from the interviews, when opposite-sex friends are not an item of marital discord it is an error to conclude that jealousy is absent or that the couple has negotiated guidelines for developing these relationships; more often it is tacitly agreed to avoid them. One of the few couples who successfully maintained such friendships was interviewed at length. George, a furniture designer, is thirty-eight. With his rugged, lean face and straight, shiny black hair he is a very attractive man. Ellen, a legal secretary, is thirty-five. A slim woman with an almost childlike appearance, Ellen looks, at most, to be in her mid-twenties. They have been married for twelve years.

George: For me a marriage can only be viable if it doesn't seriously detract from one's individuality. I don't want the kind of extreme togetherness based on insecurity that is common among married people. They even get to look alike after a while! I can't be everything to Ellen nor can she be all to me. We have shared interests along with individual interests. So if I meet another woman, say, a decorator or a designer, it is all right for me to spend time with her. We may go to a furniture show, for example. Sometimes Ellen goes to these things, too. But realistically, she can't possibly supply the same type of companionship at a designer show that I can get with another designer.

Ellen: I met an old friend, Richard, recently. We have known each other since high school. He's a musician. I'm fascinated by music—although I've never played professionally I'm just as into it as is Richard. We have a running competition about our knowledge of music. Sometimes we get together here in the apartment to listen and talk, other times we may go to a concert together. George knows I'm a frustrated musician, why should he deny me the pleasure of Richard's company? That would diminish me as a person and lessen our relationship.

All very well, but don't they ever get jealous of one another? Don't they ever wonder if the other is affair-involved? George and Ellen responded:

Ellen: Actually, four years ago I found out through a friend of mine that George did have an affair. At first I didn't believe it, but when I confronted him he admitted it. I was shocked. I felt betrayed; it was as if I had been played for a fool. Things were pretty shaky between us for a long while—probably about a year or so.

George: When I think back to that involvement, my affair made the statement, "I won't be restrained by another person's insecurity," and closer to the heart of the matter, "Ellen, dammit, stop haunting me with your damn dependence on me. Stop asking me how I spend every minute; develop yourself your own resources, don't suck from me."

Ellen: George is right, I was overly dependent. Nonetheless, that first year was very rocky. Gradually, I came to see George and myself in a different light. First of all, I've learned the "wisdom of insecurity." Both men and women have the tendency after marriage to think, "Okay, the romance is over. I can sit back now; I've won him (or her) over." This leads to stagnation. There is a healthy drive toward self-improvement that ceases after marriage. This was revitalized by the affair.

George: In the last few years, I've come to appreciate Ellen much more than previously. She has become more independent. I get a strong sense that she doesn't *need* me, but she really *wants* me. She enjoys my company but isn't dependent on it or lost without me. If I were to disappear, she would be okay and continue to live her life well. That quality is very important to me.

Ellen: Getting back to having opposite-sex friends, George and I, especially after the emotional trauma of the affair, are committed to sexual exclusivity. We are willing to risk the temptation of unrestricted companionship because not to do so seems to both of us to be an even greater, more dangerous route. Honesty, trust and commitment along with the freedom to be an individual form a stronger bond than jealousy, possessiveness and harsh restraint. The latter feels more secure but the safety, as I found, is illusory. There are no guarantees.

While not as conflicted as opposite-sex friends, same-sex friendships among the married are hardly abundant. In comparison, single men and women are more than twice as likely to have a close friend than their married counterparts. (The chances are four to one that a married person will have as a friend someone who is also married. Survey responses confirm the opinions of social scientists who have observed that we are moving toward a split society in which singles and marrieds have developed exclusionary social lives.) In most instances, the responsibilities of marriage and family are an important consideration in the depleted friendship energies of the coupled, but even in same-sex friendships, the element of jealousy enters. "It's like a slap in the face to me if my wife chooses to go out for the evening with a woman friend instead of me," one man confessed. "It's as if she is saying, 'I enjoy her company more than I do yours.'"

Although some couples viewed same-sex friends as competitors for a mate's time and affection, others were not only *not* disturbed that "outsiders" brought satisfaction to their spouse, but were relieved that they themselves were not obligated to meet every need or whim. As one woman remarked, "I wish I could find my husband a good friend. I know he's lonely. There's nobody he calls up to say hello to or just chat. It's always a business conversation. He turns to me exclusively for comforting; he'll tell me he feels tense and I rub his back and listen to his problems. But I wish he had a friend to talk to, another man in whom he could confide."

Even when extramarital friendships are maintained and accepted by a spouse, they often become diluted. In some instances, people who describe themselves as reasonably self-disclosing premaritally, become muffled. This is particularly common in sexual matters. Reviewing the survey responses on this issue, the trend toward openness, regardless of gender, favors the unmarried. In all probability an injunction is invoked because talking about sex will involve one's spouse and be viewed as a violation of the marital privacy code. For similar reasons, discussing other intimate matters with a friend is likely to bring disapproval. One woman, for example, offered that her husband stopped speaking to her for two weeks because she told a friend of his disappointment in not getting a hoped-for promotion. In other instances, shock and surprise are registered when it is found that a friend is separating without having revealed an inkling of marital strife to anyone. It seems unfortunate that sharing fears, anxieties, uncertainties and other difficult feelings pertaining to the marriage with a trusted friend is so frequently regarded disapprovingly. This type of outlet can enable a spouse to feel less burdened, less alone, and sometimes results in a new perspective.

Perhaps because of the difficulties of sustaining a serious individual friendship with an outsider of either sex, couple-to-couple friendships are the greatest source of socializing by people who are married. According to the survey, to be coupled in our society means keeping company with other couples primarily—sixty-eight percent of married people see friends in a couple context. Partners get together separately in only twenty percent of these instances, and it is more often the women than the men who see each other on a one-to-one basis. Among husbands and wives, friendship with other couples is generally accepted and viewed as nonthreatening. Even fantasies about another person's mate may be openly admitted and kidded about—so long as the friendship is couple-based and four (or more) people are interacting, the erotic elements seem to be downplayed. However, if a relationship is formed with an opposite-sex partner outside the marital pairing, once again it is frequently considered suspicious and actively or covertly discouraged.

Although the couple-to-couple relationship is the most acceptable friendship vehicle among the married, it is not without frustration. Consider the odds against finding a compatible foursome: Each person has to like two people, for a total of eight likes. The couple you like—well, you like her, and if her husband is boring, at least he's not obnoxious. Your husband, however, goes to sleep at the very sound of his voice and is angry about being trapped with them at a table for four. You pretend you want to see the two of them together; they probably get together under a similar pretense. Then there are the friends each of you believe you like but actually you feel sorry for, guilty about or somehow obliged to. You continue to inflict them on each other, keeping score: Now he owes me one, now we're even. Naturally, since few couples find both members of another couple equally palatable, compromises are made and the intimacy of close friendship is often exchanged for the superficiality of an "active social life"—cocktail parties, dinner, weekend vacations filled with tennis and more cocktail parties.

"Two may talk and one may hear," Emerson wrote in an essay on friendship, "but three cannot take part in a conversation of the most sincere and searching sort." Not to mention four or six or eight. Most of us will acknowledge that Emerson was right, but we are unable to reconcile what we know with the proscription against individualized friendship in marriage.

Friendship and the Divorce Process

First Feelings: Facing Loneliness and Friends

AT THE TURN OF THE CENTURY, divorce was a very rare occurrence, considered either an indulgence of the rich and eccentric or a desperate act of the inhumanly abused. Today, it is common for marriages to end in divorce. This fact, well known by now, is confirmed year after year as the divorce rate soars. No longer is divorce limited to the upper strata and the hopelessly disaffected; it prevails over a broad economic cross section and is based on any of myriad claims of disparity.

In the broadened arena of the divorce process, issues such as alimony, division of property, child support and custody occupy center stage. Yet, of all the negative feelings of the newly separated, none is more common or less discussed than loneliness. With all the bitterness that surrounds divorce, it is easy to forget that nearly all those who have formed a marital bond have shared countless intimacies. The relationship may have been stormy and painful, but there was caring. The dissolution of the marriage— even for those who most keenly desired the end—brings to bear on both husband and wife a void to be filled.

One husband, married fourteen years, had this to say: "I rented a small apartment. The first few weeks after our separation were hell. I didn't want to go out, I was depressed, guilty, angry. The flood of emotions overwhelmed me. Then when I started to get out, I didn't want to go back to the apartment, the silence was menacing, the air seemed heavy. It was like having hot and cold chills; first I didn't want to go out and then I would do anything to avoid going back to the apartment. I would go to lousy movies, sit in a bar all night, although I don't like to drink much or talk to dull strangers. Anything to avoid the solitude. I would go any place where I could be near other bodies, other faces, other voices. The only thing I couldn't face was my friends. Somehow I couldn't bear an explanation."

His former wife had an equally difficult time of it: "I was thrown by the attitude people had toward me as a woman alone. Some so-called friends dropped me socially. It was as if they thought it was not safe for me to be in the proximity of their husbands. I realize that divorce is increasing, but is it also contagious? The loneliness was horrid; hours on the phone or sitting in front of the television were a poor substitute for companionship—there was no one to laugh with or make comments to. I tried reading, but found myself turning pages and not remembering what I had read. One night, at bedtime, I came across one of his shirts, left in his haste to get out; how long, I wondered, will it be before all traces of his being will be erased? How long will it be before my life returns to normal? Who among my friends can I still count on? Who will offer support and a shoulder to cry on? For a while, pressed by these questions, I slept day and night. I savored sleep like a fine wine; it was my only true sanctuary."

Despite some continued friendships, many among the separated and divorced lose access to the network of social friends to which they had formerly belonged. The resulting social isolation, combined with the emotional upset of separation, gives rise to a form of loneliness that can be especially tormenting. Bereft of community, the divorced react in a variety of ways to this loneliness. Some bury themselves in activity—social service, politics, college classes, self-improvement regimens. Others, those who will not endure loneliness at any cost, may seek to rush into another romantic relationship almost immediately. Still others, particularly when they feel themselves to be sinking, clutch at the telephone for companionship. Suddenly this impersonal electronic device takes on new meaning; it becomes a life source to the world. Friends may be called endlessly under any pretense: "I hope I'm not disturbing you, but I wanted to know if the PTA meeting is still scheduled for Thursday evening." The underlying hope is that an offer will be made to get together or an invitation will be proposed, through gentle questioning, to unlock feelings—"How are things going for you?" Of course, subtlety is not a universal preference; many individuals choose to dispense with pretense and be direct: "Can I stop by this evening? I really don't want to be alone."

The reactions of friends to these requests, whether masked or overt, vary. Some withdraw, others respond quickly with a desire to help. In some measure, the difference in response corresponds to the basis of the friendship. If affection and mutual loyalty are fundamental to the bond, if the friends share segments of their personal lives with each other, the relationship is less likely to be dramatically altered by the divorce. In contrast, if marriage provided the main basis for the friendship, divorce is almost sure to weaken it. As one man remarked:

"When friends of ours separated, we were pretty uncomfortable. They broke up amid great emotional turmoil. We visited with Bill, we visited with Cindy, but we just didn't know how to talk to them. We weren't on either of their sides, but it was still very awkward. What do you say to somebody who suddenly is totally removed from your situation and so obviously pained? Is it not much different from paying a condolence call in the case of a death. What can you do? You can ask about the kids but you can't ask about the spouse—not even to mention that you've seen him or her. You feel guilty about that. You don't dare talk about your own positive family experiences for fear of heightening their misery. To say that we all have problems is condescending. If you are bold you can ask if they are dating, but that may be an embarrassing question, it may be regarded as an intrusion. Should you instead not inquire into what has happened, avoid their feelings and pretend to ignore the whole matter? If so, what the hell do you talk about? Inflation? Taxes? Lawn care? In a matter of a few weeks we were no longer in contact with our separated friends."

The awkwardness and confusion felt by those couples receiving the news of a friend's divorce are shared and magnified in the separated. Hearing the news causes strains, but the chore of delivering it is worse—and it is usually a surprise. In many instances couples whose marriages are failing continue to appear firmly linked, right up to the point of separation. Practically everyone has heard of a marital split that seemed sudden and unexpected. In reality this is never the case, but few couples are willing to drop the united façade and quarrel in public. Tact and the natural desire to avoid embarrassment dictate otherwise. Although this strategy of nonexposure may be temporarily protective, it makes it very difficult to break the news of separation:

"During that last year our marital situation grew worse by bounds. It was as if a cancer had come out of remission with a renewed ambition to destroy everything in its path. Up to that point I hadn't said anything to anybody; the most that we had exposed was an exchange of sarcastic tones. Now it could no longer be contained; I felt obliged to say something. I visited Michael and Jean, two old married friends. After the initial greetings and a bit of small talk, I simply blurted out, 'Margaret and I are separating.' After a few mumbled regrets they waited for me to take the initiative, to explain what happened. This was a moment of pure anguish for me. I had come for human warmth, I needed support, but I was ashamed and embarrassed by my plight. I felt an overwhelming sense of failure, of having screwed up a significant segment of my life.

"I didn't want to appear to them as a whiner, a weakling begging for sympathy. At the same time I sensed a need in them to know what had happened. More than morbid curiosity, it was as if they were silently saying: 'Reassure us, tell us that your marriage was nothing like ours, so that we can be sure it won't happen to us.' Finally, with my heart pounding and my brain racing at superspeed, trying to sort out my ambivalence. I started to open up. I had reached the point of no return; whatever penalties I envisioned for spilling my guts couldn't be worse than the pain of holding everything in. Out it came, in a gush as unceasing as a waterfall, anger, grief and guilt. I needed that release and I'm glad it occurred, but I hardly see Michael and Jean anymore; we've drawn away from each other."

As with this man, many individuals approach the grim chore of telling married friends of their separation with mixed feelings. Pulled toward disclosure by the need for release, tugged back toward saying little or nothing by the anticipated self-denigration of the task, about one man in five and one woman in three offers a detailed explanation to married friends. The large majority of recently separated save the detailed accounts for a close relative or a dear friend—if such a person exists. About fifteen percent go it alone, volunteering the particulars of their plight to no one.

There are two important factors that bear on these findings. First, as we have seen, it is often the case that the term "friend" is applied loosely among couples. More accurately, when couples speak of their couple-to-couple friendships, they are usually referring to social acquaintances, not true intimates. Consequently, low self-disclosure is not surprising in a time of crisis; it is simply an extension of the general tone of the relationship. Second, most social circles have an underlying set of standards that determine what kind of behavior is viewed as desirable and what is deemed unacceptable. Discussing this issue with the separated and divorced, it was clear that these standards are given consideration. In some friendship groups, divorce may be accepted and even encouraged as a preferred form of behavior. Several of the group members may be remarried and are quite familiar with the divorce process. In other instances, the climate may be harshly judgmental. Sticking with a problem, self-sacrifice for the sake of the children and forsaking individual happiness may be reinforced. In such groups, revealing marital discord or announcing a separation is difficult enough. Giving an intimate account is paramount to masochism.

While a minority of men and women choose complete silence and others discuss the minutiae of their separation openly, the great majority at least inform those with whom they have regular contact: "When Jeffrey and I separated I felt compelled to tell the people in my office. Not saying anything would be an affront. We do things together, they've met my children; to allow them to continue believing that I was married would feel fraudulent. I would feel burdened by this 'dark' secret. It was not pleasant, but I decided I would rather have it out in the open than to have them find out and be whispering about it behind my back. One day, I went to lunch with two women I am friendly with and was asked, 'How's things?' I told them Jeffrey and I had split. They were shocked, but after a few minutes of discussion and an offer of a blind date—which I took a raincheck on—we settled down to our usual talk of politics, books, the children and mutual interests."

Whatever the potential drawbacks of broaching the subject of a recent separation—embarrassment, rejection, awkwardness, shame and the like—practically all of those interviewed agreed that it is an important step to take. During the period between the initial separation and the completion of the divorce, an emotional digestion process begins. Acknowledging the separation personally and reinforcing it publicly is the first step toward independence and a critical event in the reorganization of one's life.

Emotional Reactions of Friends: Second Phase

The initial response of friends, as noted earlier, is often one of surprise followed by awkwardness. But rather soon these inaugural reactions begin to fade and a more differentiated, complex variety present themselves. Some friends continue to be welcoming, others begin to feel burdened by the weight of the complaints being aired. Some seem frightened of the divorced person and act as if he or she had a communicable disease. Often, at the base of such an anxiety response is a friend's unsatisfactory marriage. Divorce is a dramatic act having the power to stir those surrounding the event, if only momentarily, to take another look at their own marriages. As one woman, married ten years, disclosed:

"When I heard that Diana was separated and was delighted in her newfound freedom, I was really alarmed. I purposely avoided her because I knew that I should be doing the same thing and did not have the courage. My hopes for fulfillment in my marriage were dashed long ago. I rationalized that divorce was hell and that I was doing the right thing by sticking with my husband even though there was hardly anything between us. Diana, by extricating herself from a similar situation and rediscovering her well-being, challenged my complacency. I could have tolerated our relationship much more easily if she wasn't having such a good time! If only being single didn't bring her so much joy; if only it didn't confront me with an option I try to pretend doesn't exist."

In some instances close friends of many years were unable to tolerate the separation, as was the case with the woman quoted above, while casual friends may continue to be warm and understanding. A close friend may be so gripped by identification with the process that he or she can become condemning, rude or even hostile. Some may feel oppressively protective; they may attend to the separated as if he or she is a gravely wounded animal in need of round-the-clock care. Concomitantly with this smothering response, there is often a preoccupation with the details of the marital discord and separation. The friend may continuously talk about it, seek more information and endlessly probe until it becomes unbearable to even the most tolerant of individuals.

And, as with all relationships, there is often within them a disturbing ambivalence. While a friend may sympathize with the suffering and pain of the divorced, he or she may also experience pleasure. This is more likely to occur when envy, which loomed silently in the background of the relationship, suddenly surfaces. Perhaps the divorced individual is favored with wealth or unusual talent or a highly desired position; the failure of his or her marriage may be taken to balance the scales of self-esteem between rivalrous friends: "Sure, he's successful," a junior executive remarked of his divorcing friend, "but he achieved what he has at the expense of his family; he's not really happy."

One reaction particularly troublesome to newly separated women is a veiled or direct sexual overture from male friends. Numerous women protested that quite without provocation one or more husbands among their friends came on to them sexually. Some exploitative men are dismayingly crass in their solicitations. Such a man may approach a woman friend and ask her bluntly whether she will go to bed with him. In contrast, another kind of exploiter may slowly and patiently devote himself to being helpful; perhaps he may stop over after work "to see if everything is alright"; he may call frequently or offer to take the woman out for a drink. By his purposeful and strategically measured attention he hopes gradually to ready an acceptance to a discreet affair.

Irene Ramsey felt panic-stricken when her husband walked out in the middle of their vacation. Returning to her hotel room after a day of shopping, she found his brief note:

I've decided that our marriage is futile. We are only hurting each other by continuing. I will be packed and out of the house by the time you return home.

Mike

Irene arrived in New York late Sunday evening and was due at her busy personnel office on Monday morning. Caught up in the hurly-burly of work, her separation anxiety almost disappeared; it didn't come back until the evening. This same sequence of distraction and anxiety was repeated on Tuesday and continued each day in what seemed to be an endless pattern. When Irene came home on Friday she decided not to spend another anxiety-filled evening alone; instead she visited a married friend who lived in the neighborhood.

"I had been fairly close with Betty for three years. I spoke to her quite candidly about my feelings, my fears and guilt. I felt as if the words 'I am a failure' were emblazoned on my forehead for all who passed to read. I revealed my frustration with Mike's lack of sexual desire and the difficulties we had had in that regard. I told her I was simply unable to accept the lack of womanliness I felt by his continuing lack of sexual interest. As far as I was concerned I had forced the separation because of the pressure I exerted—but I really believed that the separation might make him change in some way. Perhaps it would free him for an affair—maybe that would awaken his sexuality. Who knows? I certainly fantasized an affair often enough. I desperately wanted to feel desired again. I needed to feel more like a woman. Having a sibling relationship with my husband was demoralizing. All in all, I poured my heart out in great detail and found Betty to be quite supportive.

"Soon after that conversation with Betty I received a call from her husband, Tom. He expressed his concern and was warm and protective. His manner seemed quite genuine, he acted as if he really cared. I was touched. For the next few weeks he would call periodically and inquire how things were going. At one point he asked if I was dating and I told him I hadn't worked up the courage for that yet. One day about two months after Mike had left, I stopped by Betty's to return a book I had borrowed. Unexpectedly, Tom was there; he had taken the day off to finish painting the house. Betty was out for the day. He offered me a drink, which I accepted although I felt a little funny being there alone with him. But I reasoned that we had a brother-sister relationship—he had never been flirtatious—and he had been so supportive that to run out without being social might be offensive.

"At first our conversation was more of the usual, you know, 'Hello, how are you? What have you been up to?' Then he started pawing at me and said—I'll never forget how sleazy he looked at that moment—'you poor thing, you must really be hurting. You haven't felt like a woman for so long!' Obviously, he had nominated himself as my redeemer. My anger was immediate. 'You no good son-of-a-bitch,' I screamed. 'I'm friends with your wife. All the while you pretended to really care. Don't you ever touch me or contact me again!' This is unbelievable, but that arrogant bastard persisted. He said, 'Come on, Irene. Betty told me about you and Mike. It would be a release, you'd feel better about yourself!' With that I shoved him away from me so hard that he fell back over the couch; I went home and threw up. I felt totally degraded."

Some wives, sensitive to the possibility that their spouse may develop a sudden libidinous interest in a divorced woman and offer to become "surrogate husband," purposely discourage friendly relations. With divorced or separated men, a similar if not as frequent phenomenon occurs. One man, friendly with several married women, was told quite directly and firmly by husbands to stay away. Another man reported an incident in which a close friend's wife came by his apartment late one evening to discuss her marriage. Soon after she arrived, obviously a bit tipsy, she announced that her husband was out of town and that she wanted to stay over. The man had no desire to jeopardize his long-standing friendship and sent the woman home.

In sum, whether friends respond with anxiety, lust, pleasure, withdrawal or understanding seems to be a function of many factors. The reactions of friends depend as much on their own psyche, the state of their own marriage or expectations for marriage as on the history of the friendship. Consequently, a long-term friendship may be shattered by the divorce process while a more recent alliance may remain intact. This may occur simply because the divorce process had evoked a strong, disruptive reaction in the older friend. Of course, there are other issues that enter into this complex arena which remains to be discussed: the way the broken marriage ended, conflicts of loyalty and changes in life style. These matters notwithstanding, a divorce can represent a threat, fulfillment of a hidden wish, a disillusionment or an emotional loss. Talking with people about divorce, it became increasingly apparent that these factors—individual views of the divorce, rather than the divorce itself—are crucial for the divorcing parties to consider in their effort to understand why some friends suffer, others take flight or deny being affected and still others supply emotional aid.

Conflicts of Loyalty

In all too many instances, divorce is a grim process including the breakup of the home, disputes over the division of property and a fierce struggle to win over the children; strong feelings of hostility and rancor in a separating couple are common. For friends, this may lead to a conflict over allegiances. With whom does the friend side? Some friends will ally themselves with one of the separated, some will try to maintain a strict neutrality and others are primarily concerned with the welfare of the children involved. In the more amiable separations—an admirable but infrequent occurrence—taking sides is a minor issue. In the most bitter uncouplings—those that involve the discovery of an extra-marital affair, a rivalrous lover—the urge to destroy the sexual wanderer sometimes becomes overwhelming. Formerly gentle spouses can turn into seething monsters, taking out and exposing family skeletons in order to "teach the son-of-a-bitch a lesson." Inevitably, friends figure in the wrath.

Alice Fay is an attractive woman in her early forties. During the fifteen years she was married to Arnold, she thought they had a satisfactory marriage. But now, four years after her divorce, she recalls that during the last three years of the marriage, she and her husband only slept together once or twice a month—usually after Arnold had had a few drinks. Alice accepted their deteriorating sex life as the natural consequence of many years together, until one of her "kind" friends told her that Arnold's pleasure and interests lay elsewhere. The weeks that followed were such agony for both that even before the divorce proceedings were underway, Arnold moved out. Alice was so engulfed in hurt and so intent on revenge that Arnold could not even talk to her. His tone of voice, a gesture, was enough to set her off in a violent rage.

"The hatred I felt for Arnold ran deep. The chill I experienced in his presence was devastating. It was over three years before we were able to treat each other casually and lightly. For me, those years were filled with self-pity and hate. The thought that he had a lover waiting in the wings for the final decree drove me wild. To think that I trusted him all those years. I felt so exposed, so vulnerable, betrayed. I felt as if someone had cut me open and pulled out my insides. My sleep was disturbed for months, I would wake up shaking in the night, sometimes I threw up. When I thought of him with her, I was absolutely beside myself. All that we had worked for—he was making a good living; we had grown up together. I sacrificed, he sacrificed—now she, rather than I, was to savor the rewards of those difficult years. I couldn't accept the injustice! I was consumed with revenge. I thought of turning him in to the IRS for tax fraud. I considered blackmail, disfigurement, murder. I settled for isolating him completely from our community of friends. I started a fervent campaign to turn them against him by presenting an image of him as an out-and-out culprit, a callous, nonfeeling, indifferent bastard.

"The reaction of our friends was varied. 'I told you so,' one managed. 'My husband did the same thing and I have never forgiven him.' 'My husband plays around a bit but so do I,' another remarked casually. 'What you need is a real son-of-a-bitch lawyer,' my close friend Martha offered. What I wanted and what I was getting was for all of our mutual friends to gang up on him. I made it quite clear that if they saw him socially they could not continue to be my friend. If I heard that one of our so-called friends was seeing him, having him to dinner or something, that traitor now became the enemy. I would not accept the explanation that the person liked both of us, together and individually, as human beings, and the fact that we had parted—however unhappily—in no way altered their affection for either of us. They had to make a choice; I not only solicited their exclusive loyalty, I demanded it. There was nothing sweeter to my ears than hearing my friends tell me what a total slob or brute Arnold was to ruin our marriage over some whore. When my friend Martha told me that Arnold tried joining her and her husband's table at a restaurant and she insisted that he leave, I was delighted. It seems that Arnold was so startled that at first he refused. Martha, no powder puff herself, called the manager and had him ordered away from the table in a cloud of embarrassment. This is the kind of drama I relished."

However gratifying "taking sides" may be to the person whose cause is being championed, it practically always does more harm than good. This is not to say that discussions of sensitive issues with friends always prove destructive. Numerous people attested to the value of their friends at this time of crisis in their lives. But, as one man wisely stated, "Friends are hardly ever objective about marriage problems; stick to the support they offer and regard their advice and opinions with a grain of salt." Previous to an actual split, friends may speed the movement toward divorce by acting as judges and reinforcing feelings of injustice, hurt and guilt. After an actual separation, denunciations by friends only serve to polarize the couple and interfere with their efforts to communicate and sensibly sort out their situation.

One rarely considered result of the mustering of battle lines is the effect on the children. When friends withdraw, as they often do rather than engage in a tug-of-war over loyalties, the children may miss their presence. It is no exaggeration to say that the center of a child's world is his or her family. The family determines social relations, shapes adaptive habits and influences personal well-being. When this mainstay collapses, the youngster's sense of self and security is threatened. The absence of familiar faces in the form of his or her parents' friends (and perhaps broken relationships with their children) is a further disruption. The intensity of change to be mastered is increased; parents' friends and their children often provide important relationships. Loss of these deprives the child of a sense of continuity; for the child who feels his or her "badness" was responsible for the divorce, the withdrawal of friends may even reinforce these suspicions. In contrast, if friends aren't used as weapons, they can be helpful to the child. They might provide a substitute for an absent parent, make the disrupted home less lonely and sad. A nineteen-year-old woman whose parents were divorced when she was twelve recalls the experience:

"My parents fought over everything. And when they separated they fought over their friends. They treated them as possessions to divide up. As a result, most of their friends deserted them. Unfortunately, I also lost many of my friends because of the strain between their parents and mine. To this day, I do not forgive my parents for that. I was painfully lonely and hurt by them. I can accept their getting a divorce, but the way they acted after the separation drove everyone away and showed absolutely no concern for me. I lost everything—my father, my friends, the comfort of some of their friends who were like relatives to me."

Yet, for all the disadvantages of involving friends in the divorce battle, evidence that it occurs with some frequency was gleaned from in-depth interviews. Interestingly, divorced wives more than their ex-partners seem to reach for this weapon. If men are less prone to assemble loyal forces, however, it is unlikely to be the result of pure nobility. Rather, it is probably because they are much more indisposed to public emotion than women; they are more inclined to dramatize their battle and soothe their wounds in bars, with strangers.

Staying Together While Coming Apart: Friendships Between Former Mates

Without doubt, the dissolution of a marriage strains the ties of camaraderie between the divorce-involved and their friends. It is in this context of a tenuous social network that the divorced face the major task of reshaping their lives. Equally as important, particularly while practical matters exist between ex-spouses—alimony, which signifies the penalty of failure, and children, flesh-and-blood reminders of the former attachment—is a laying to rest of personal grievances. "Can we be civilized about this?" a former couple ask each other. "Can we act sensibly?" they wonder silently. "Or are we to be imprisoned by out mutual venom in a web of ill will?"

How do former spouses cope with each other? Is it possible for them to achieve a friendship? After all, they have a bank of stored memories, good as well as bad; in addition to the lasting influence of shared experiences, most have a lingering feeling of familial concern. Despite these bonds, friendship is usually not even considered. Indeed, most want as little as possible to do with each other. Far from feeling friendly, at one point or another, usually in a moment of desperation—when guilt and anger press to unbearable limits—they may seek relief by fantasizing the demise of their antagonist. "I wish," one tormented woman sighed, "he would drop dead—painlessly, but instantly and thoroughly!"

Beyond wishful thinking, moving away is often considered as a solution. Relocating cannot erase past memories, but if the relationship is combative it can halt the accumulation of new daily assaults. However, although it does provide a solution of sorts, reestablishing oneself elsewhere has serious drawbacks. If children are involved, the noncustodial parent, in effect, loses contact with them. Emotionally this is often traumatic. Legally, the custodial parent may be restrained from a long-distance move. Combine these factors with the loss of friends and family, the necessity of starting over in a new job and living in unfamiliar surroundings, and the psychological impact is almost intolerable. Because of the children, out of loneliness or a fear of rootlessness —for all the reasons already mentioned—husbands and wives continue to exist in each other's lives, and opportunities for interacting remain plentiful. Feelings are likely to be mixed about these interactions and may alternate between friendship and animosity, or the two may be present simultaneously as in the man or woman who experiences both distress and relief upon the notice of a spouse's impending remarriage.

Although there are few societal safeguards against the psychological abuse a formerly married couple may engage in, for most the feelings of anger, guilt and hurt gradually shrivel. The average duration appears to be about two years—a difficult and seemingly endless period when what one desires is immediate cessation. Yet there are no shortcuts. It took time to weave so complicated a relationship and, despite impatience, the time requirement refuses to yield to emotional discomfort.

Along with time, disengagement from a former attachment depends to some degree on external circumstances. Young people who have former spouses, children and heavy support payments are likely to have more problems than older couples whose children are grown and living elsewhere. If a former partner is no longer alive, or lives a great distance away, relationships are simplified. Couples, without children, who both have careers can more easily disentangle their involvement, particularly if there is no demand for alimony, and can go their very separate ways. Community acceptance, including supportive rather than provocative intervention from friends, and neutrality on the part of former in-laws can also help to dissipate animosity.

Beyond circumstantial factors—often lying outside our locus of control—are psychological issues. For some people—those who married in order to avoid becoming autonomous individuals, the insecure, and those who are afraid to meet others—the steps toward inner rehabilitation and letting go are seriously impeded. To become an individual, to loosen the habit of seeing oneself as part of a couple, requires learning to live without somebody to lean on. Some people have forgotten how to do it; others have never learned. Both the friends and the former spouse of these people are likely to be pestered and choked for months and even years with too heavy a claim on their sympathies.

Those who develop a stronger sense of security, who grow toward autonomy, may, in time, form an essentially neutral attitude toward their ex-spouse—where bitterness and fear have either vanished or are held within manageable bounds. In some people, this neutrality can even progress into a friendship. Through familiarity and a common bond with the person who was so much a part of one's life, and knowing that day-to-day friction no longer exists, a gradual friendliness begins to emerge. A commercial artist, forty-two, divorced four years and now remarried, reports:

"Celia, my former wife, and I were college classmates. We married in our senior year because we wanted to live together; to do so without being married would have scandalized our parents and society twenty years ago. Over the years we gradually became disenchanted with each other. By the time we thought of doing something about it, it was too late. We couldn't recapture the relationship and mutually decided to end it. For the first three years of our separation, it was difficult for both of us; the traits of one of us used to trigger hostility in the other. Gradually, though, these things began to have less impact. These days we actually see a great deal of each other. In some ways, we may even be more honest and warm than when we were married. Not having the day-to-day grind helps. It also helps that we have both found ourselves and we are happy with our lives. We see each other or call to discuss things concerning our son Paul, about once or twice a week. Politics, interesting things that have occurred, gossip about mutual friends, are also part of our conversation. Occasionally, once a month or so, Celia and I even meet for lunch. We have even been together as a foursome, Celia and her husband and my wife, Lisa, and I, to have a drink together. It is always pleasant and friendly—after all, we enjoy each other's company and bygones are bygones."

This kind of interaction, where ex-mates see each other socially and consider themselves friends, is relatively rare. It was reported by a mere five percent of formerly married survey respondents. In no case had the initial separation occurred less than two years previous. More often, if formerly married couples no longer *need* their ex-spouses—if they have rebuilt their lives so as to meet their emotional and social needs through others—they may be cordial but not close. Theirs is not a real friendship of the kind in which people seek each other out because they want to be together, but rather a friendliness characterized by an exchange of holiday greetings, a feeling of good will, sympathetic interest and so on. No longer directed by a worn-out script of the past, they desire to treat each other fairly; they do not wish to socialize, but they are not uncomfortable with each other. Ideally, it would be nice if more ex-mates could be friends, but considering the dark emotions many get caught up in—hate, guilt, fear—achieving neutrality appears to be a noble compromise.

New Alignments

Since most of the friendships of married people depend on their marital status, separation frequently disconnects them from their network of friends. Nearly three-quarters of the separated or divorced respondents stated that after one year their most active friendships were not with couples they had socialized with previously. Yet, despite this sharp decline in coupled friends, in many instances the relationships were not completely shattered. If the spouse was not an essential link to the relationship, some of the separated retained limited friendships with the same-sex spouse of the couples they had known: Women may visit with married friends for an afternoon; men may see each other at business, for lunch or as partners in sporting activities.

As for more social occasions with these married friends, the separated individual is likely to feel out of place—half a couple in a roomful of couples. "My concerns," a recently separated woman remarked, "are the problems of being a single parent, difficulties with loneliness and dating. These matters are foreign to my married friends. I want friends who have something to say about these pressing problems. I'm restless with what I now regard as the small talk of my married friends." The married, too, as we have seen, often feel a strain with this familiar person who is now different.

There are a multitude of reasons for the melting away of relationships with married friends. In addition to psychological factors—disruptive emotional reactions, conflicts of loyalty and growing differences in life style—are practical matters. That is, changing one's friends is not entirely the result of being rejected by them or even of having decided to reject them. The change may come about merely because getting together has become more problematic: A change of residence for the separated man is practically inevitable; the separated woman very often may begin paid employment and, consequently, has less time for socializing. As a forty-two-year-old woman explained:

"After our separation it was mandatory for me to return to work. Without working I could never afford to keep the house and my sons would only suffer another dramatic change. So, rather than move, I chose to take a full-time job. Now I had full responsibility for the house—cooking, cleaning, shopping and laundry—and I didn't return home until six in the evening. After supper I didn't know where to start: going over homework, housework, giving the boys attention. It was exhausting. On top of it all, I was desperately lonely, but when my friends called I hardly had time to talk with them, no less see them. It was very, very frustrating."

Divorce need not be the signal that friendships have come to a halt and are never to be resumed. For one thing, although most of the separated lose access to their network of married friends, some remain in touch with one or two couples and may even become closer to them than they had been when they were married. Second, there are friendly contacts with same-sex members of the married couples that had formerly been friends. There may also be an intimate friend, married or unmarried. What's more, most men and women succeed in the face of broken marriages to rebuild their social life. Gradually, out of necessity, their lives move toward coherence and order.

Eventually, over eighty percent of those who were divorced three or more years developed a new network of friends. In fact, although only one in five persons who have been divorced made new friends in less than a year, the percentage increases to three out of five between the first and second year; by the end of the third year four out of five have found new friends. A minority take longer and some, less than one-fifth, even after three years, did not make new friends. In discussions with the divorced, the term "friend," it should be noted, did not necessarily suggest great intimacy of relationship; often they were referring to someone to do things with, a group of individuals who were central to their new social network.

Are demographic factors—age, sex, religion, education, locality and parental status—associated with the forming of these new friendships? A careful screening of the data yields a qualified yes. Women, significantly more than men, make new friends faster—regardless of whether or not they have children. Common sense tells us that having children would tie women down—and it does—but apparently the desire for companionship is a strong incentive to work out the practical problems of time and organization.

For both men and women, income, level of education, religion and age do not shed light on the rate at which new friendships are acquired or whether they are made at all. Young and old, rich and poor, college professor and laborer, Catholic, Protestant and Jew stand an equal chance of forming a new friendship network. While these variables proved to be insignificant, locality revealed itself to be of consequence. More than any other circumstantial factor, living in a small town appears to be a handicap. Decidedly, those individuals who succeeded at rebuilding their friendship network most rapidly more often resided in large metropolitan areas. It seems that even if the reputation of our cities as cold and impersonal is true, the large number of formerly married and the new social acceptability of divorce in these areas combine to counteract unfriendliness and produce what is, in effect, a giant meeting place for the separated and divorced.

Some of the separated and divorced not only recoup their friendship losses but feel they have developed a richer social life and better friends than they had when they were married. An important factor here is the individual's willingness to participate in the marketplace of unattached people. One woman in her early forties described her experience:

"When I was married we lived in a stuffy family community. It seemed that our entire neighborhood was in bed by eleven. On weekends after an evening of bridge, dinner out or a movie, lights went out about midnight. When my marriage broke up I found myself to be the object of my friends' pity and, sometimes, their suspicion. After a while their reactions to me and the lack of opportunity to meet new people convinced me to move closer to the city. I thought a fresh start in a new but not totally unfamiliar place would do me a world of good. Dana, my daughter, was reluctant at first but finally she agreed. After we got settled in our new place, I began going to public events, joining organizations. I pursued all kinds of social opportunities. Dana made friends quickly at school. She adjusted beautifully. I deliberately became involved with groups of other unattached people such as Parents Without Partners. Some of the people I met at PWP were not easy to relate to. Their conversations were so predictable it was tiresome: horror stories of divorce, problems with children and tales of financial woe were not exactly my idea of an evening out. But despite some real losers, I met some very nice people.

"There are two people I met with whom I feel particularly close. One is Gail, a delight to talk to. She comes to the house and we really confide in each other and give each other support. We're each other's psychologists. She tells me how terrific I am and I tell her how terrific she is. There is something very fine and sturdy about Gail. She's a woman who has been through an awful lot and not only survived but prospered. I have really learned something about womanhood from her. Mary Alice is another gem. I met her at a singles' tennis evening. Over a period of several months we've gotten together quite often. One night, very late, she called me in obvious distress. She found out she was pregnant and was having a very difficult time dealing with the prospect of abortion. Her 'boyfriend' didn't want to take time off from work to accompany her to the clinic, so I went instead. It was a very trying time, but I'm glad I came through for her; we're still very close even though we both have steady men in our lives now."

In addition to finding new same-sex friends as in the instance above, some among the separated form opposite-sex friendships for the first time in many years. At a time when memories of a disappointing marital experience are still at issue, opposite-sex friends can be a useful element in the healing process. When emotions are wounded, there is, as with a broken limb, a period of knitting during which isolation is required; but if the limb is to grow strong again, it must be tested. Our feelings operate in similar fashion: We need to try them out, exercise them, even if cautiously at first, in order that they may return, in time, to full functioning. Aside from companionship and stability in a world where one-night stands are not uncommon, a relationship with someone of the other sex in which there is no romantic interest can provide a bridge, an emotionally safe step toward developing new romantic associations.

There are no typical divorced people and very few formulas for developing new friendships. Being receptive and friendly, living in an area where opportunities for meeting people exist and pursuing these opportunities help. Working to overcome the negative emotions of the previous marriage and divorce—the anger, jealousy, guilt, plots of revenge and loneliness that burst in and out of daily experience—is essential to being open to new relationships. Given some success at these tasks, it is probable that the divorced individual will find membership in a new community of friends. In all likelihood most friends in the group will be unmarried, and social life with them will be different but not necessarily inferior to what had been maintained during the days of marriage. And, as is becoming well known, within a few years the great majority of the divorced will remarry. Here again, the friendship circle is likely to undergo yet another reshuffling.

Friendship and Fame

WHENEVER A FAMOUS PERSON appears in public—on the street, in a restaurant, at a theater—he or she is stared at and wondered about. Many of us are curious about the life styles of those in the public eye. Magazines such as *People* and *Us* depend on our celebrity thirst; they titillate us with a glimpse into the lives of the famous. Gossip columnists have, through the famous, become public figures themselves, and talk shows thrive on our enduring interest in the celebrated. Fame has captured the American psyche and is continually fed, promoted and exploited by highly successful newspapers, magazines and television programs. As Studs Terkel in a review of *Celebrity Register* (*The Nation*, February 23, 1974) observed of most of us, the anonymous millions:

> ". . . there is a surrogate life to be daily lived. It makes the day go faster for Teddy, the doorman, who watches the human traffic at a Loop office build-

156

ing. 'Hey,' there's a fever to his usual monotone 'who was that just come in? I seen that face, I know. He's supposed to be somebody famous.' It matters little whether the face, probably one that has appeared on a TV talk show, represents a commercial, a political idea, an art, a science or a call house—for Teddy it is enough. Two, three such winners a week and he has it made.

"Others, less fortunate, must make do with images on the TV screen. On rare occasions, when the image in some occult manner materializes on the street, at the airport or in some lucky somebody's cab, the anonymous one experiences the shock of recognition. If the face is Bill Russell's or, God willing, Charlton Heston's, it may provide conversation for an otherwise lost weekend. In any event, it helps the faceless survive the day."

And while we, the "faceless," are confronted with a daily media blitz, our fascination with the lives of the famous continues undaunted. "What is he (she) really like?" is a question asked endlessly. Everyone seems to want something from celebrities; their personal lives are complicated because of the demands made of them. As a consequence of living life in the fast lane, the friendship experience of celebrities is suspect. Many of us, while envying the glamor of the famous, believe their lives to be void of solid friendships. Erica Jong, for example, speaking of her friendships after the enormous success of her novel *Fear of Flying*, in an *Esquire* interview (May 1977) stated: "My writer friends, particularly the ones with whom I used to swap manuscripts when we were all unpublished, have fallen away in the last two years. Since I've been successful, many of them do not wish me well. To put it mildly, I think they'd like me to fall through an open manhole and disappear." Do famous people lose friends to success? Is life really lonelier at the top? To find out, I decided to ask a few who have been there about their friendship experiences.

ELI WALLACH, *Actor*

"You know, there's an old doggerel verse, a little poem that goes 'a friend is not a fellow who's taken in by sham, a friend is one who knows your faults and doesn't give a damn.' A good friend is someone who, even if you've been away a long time and haven't been in touch, can pick up where we left off and doesn't waste time asking for explanations. I have several such good friends. I'm spending time with an old friend now, Peter Witt. He was my agent for twenty-five years and although he has given up being an agent, we still have interest in each other. He is spending the weekend with me.

"My closest friend was David Stewart, who died shortly after World War II. We met at the Neighborhood Playhouse, an acting school. I remember one incident with David in particular. To prove he could take it, he joined the paratroopers. I was in Africa before he arrived. Being in the Medics, I received a manifest of the people coming in and was aware of his landing. The incoming troops landed and marched through the town where I was stationed—Casablanca. They had stuck David out in a field somewhere and I recall walking through the field and seeing him. I was an officer and he was an enlisted man. He came running toward me with his arms outstretched and I thought 'Oh my God, what do I do? Does he have to salute?' The protocol of the Army was ingrained and formal. I saw David often, and we remained friends for many years. But he died. He was a very close friend.

"I have a friend, a musician. We had a sad misunderstanding about the rental of my summer house. I had to renege on it and he quite understandably didn't talk to me for two years. The process of healing was very delicate, and it took a lot of time until all those things that interfered with the friendship originally were finally eroded. Now we are friends again. It is an intriguing process resuming a damaged relationship. My wife (Anne Jackson) is doing a play called *Slightly Delayed* with Geraldine

Paige. It involves two people in a small airport in 1927, waiting for the plane to be serviced for takeoff. Another couple comes in and they, coincidentally, are the former spouses of the first couple. The play investigates what happened to their relationships, what they feel now toward each other. It is fascinating.

"My closest friend is my wife. I turn to her in times of stress. She's a rock, she's a very strong woman and very supportive. She's both a wife and a friend. One of the most difficult times, in retrospect, was during the McCarthy era. Imagine not being able to work for speaking your mind. Imagine if you were told you would never work again in your chosen field for your views—if you opposed the Vietnam war, for instance, and said so outspokenly, it would be terribly sad if that determined your fitness for work. My good friend, Zero Mostel, suffered through this ugly period. He was a good man, a dear friend.

"Maureen Stapleton—we did the *Rose Tattoo* together in the 1950s—is my closest friend. (I consider myself a liberated man in this regard. The fact of a person being male or female does not at all determine my friendship preference.) Fortunately, unlike the motion-picture business, theater people become family. Take *Mr. Roberts*, for example; I worked in that play for two years with Henry Fonda. We've known each other for twenty-five years. I feel Hank is a friend of mine. He's a man with whom I could exchange ideas. I can talk openly with him. Neither of us feels competitive or threatened by each other. Alan Arkin and I did a play together. Alan is having a very special go at it now, I feel pleased that my friend is doing well. The movies are different. You ride very high and can go very low. It is more competitive, it is a difficult business.

"To all of us in the entertainment field—whether it be motion pictures, television or theater—the issue of being used, of being courted for our celebrity status can occur but it is not really a problem which affects my friendships. I can sense that sort of thing very quickly and I put a stop to it. It's similar to trying to butter up to some multimillionaire in the hope that he might die and leave you millions. Being a good businessman and a shrewd judge of character, he would probably sense why a person is interested in him. As an actor, I am acutely aware of motives and drives that people have—very, very sharply so. It's like a blind person who has developed another sense. I think actors have that refined perception, consequently I can clearly sense when I am being used and I don't allow it.

"In contrast to the popular view of superficial friendships and being used by hangers on, many actors, myself included, are very happy with the people they know and the friendships they've formed. My brother just retired at age seventy and he was given a surprise party. Both my wife and I were moved by the adoration that people had for him. Everyone got up and made these flowery, laudatory speeches. It may have sounded as if he were being eulogized, because my brother said he was delighted to be alive to hear all those wonderful things. As my brother was speaking, surrounded by all those adoring people, I wondered what it will be like when I retire or die. You know, you get to an age when you read the obituaries—I do. I sometimes wonder what will be said about me. People are important to me. I can't help wondering, I've gone to so many funerals in recent years; many of my good friends are gone. I lost a very wonderful friend not long ago. He was outspoken, candid and loving. It was astounding to see how many people were affected by this man. He had pride, dignity and a concern for others. Those are qualities that I admire in a person. These qualities rather than complete self-involvement move me. When I was growing up people used to huddle together, there was a real caring for each other. There may be less of that now. I miss it."

GAEL GREENE, *Food Critic, Journalist and Author of the Best-Selling Novel*, Blue Skies, No Candy

"My priority has always been my life. My life comes before my work, although, admittedly, my life and my work blur and become one. There is no doubt that love and the demands of love can always get me away from the typewriter. My friends are very much a part of my life. Friends are essential to me. I spend hours advancing the cause or the work of a friend. Of course, such virtue is rarely ever purely altruistic. I would love to be able to count on my friends as they can count on me. What I've learned, though, is that not everyone has the time or the spirit to give equally or in the same ways. I've come to see people's differences—how differently we love, how differently we communicate our caring—and to accept that. Sometimes it's maddening. I've discovered there is no such thing as 'If you loved me, you would read my mind.' When I want something, I try to say so—but I love it when my needs are anticipated and indulged.

My husband and I were divorced in 1974, but he continues to be one of my closest friends. In crisis or in joy I always call him. If things are happening that require advice, I'm afraid I may actually call him several times in a day. He calls me for cooking instructions, to deliver good news and sometimes when he is down. We speak often. Many friends who were close to us both have managed to remain friends with both of us. Because we stayed friends, people did not feel forced to take sides.

"Many men with whom I have been romantically involved remain friends. These men who came into my life after my marriage and have remained close even though the intense romance has ended. The friendship may even become more loving than the romance. Some people aren't able to handle intimacy well. That's what my new novel, *The Sexual Archives of Dr. Barney Kincaid*, is about—the difficulties of romantic intimacy. I'm an incurable romantic. And I love to be in love. But I live through periods without romance, and I could not survive without friendship.

"Although I have close male friends, my very closest, most endearing friends have always been women. I have a very special close friend that I speak to practically every day. We've known each other for about eight years. We share the same passion for great food and adventure. I knew we were soul mates when, after meeting her in New York at a dinner, I unexpectedly ran into her in three different restaurants in France in two weeks. I thought to myself that crossing paths that many times in so short a period must mean something. I love her brightness and I love her optimism. She's one of those people who, as a child, was constantly told how wonderful she was, and she grew up believing it—not in an arrogant or conceited way but with a cheerful vibrance. She expects life to work and everything to turn out for the best. The expectation tends to enhance the reality. It's wonderful to be around someone like that. She's patient, wise, intelligent, generous with her time and loving enough to offer advice and criticism.

"Many of my friends are ambitious and accomplished. Some are more successful than I and some are less successful. I am not aware of having lost any friends because of my own success. There may be acquaintances who are serious writers who liked me better as a restaurant writer than as a novelist. Perhaps we might have been friendlier at one time or another and the publication of my novel *Blue Skies, No Candy* led to a coolness. I don't know for sure. I doubt it. I think in the instance of a blockbuster best-seller, like Erica Jong's book, it may be harder to maintain friendships. There is so much publicity and hoopla, it is difficult on friends. I suppose envy can be destructive. An insecure friend may imagine you will change and reject you first, before you get a chance to reject him or her. In my case, I had financial success but several bad reviews that made me the underdog and therefore people were kinder. They needn't feel threatened. The truth is: Someone else's victory takes nothing away from you. When Mario Puzo got $2 million for paperback rights to his new novel, I was delighted. 'Next time it could be me,' I thought. I've tried very hard to maintain my relationships with those people who've made it in such a grand way that they have been woven into another world. For the most part, I've succeeded."

ROBERT STACK, *Actor*

"I have a very strange background with regard to friendship. I had a close association with many people who became somewhat like surrogate fathers because when I was a small child my mother and father divorced and I went to Paris with my mother, who was studying voice. When I came back to America at age seven, I spoke only French and Italian. That was very difficult. My brother had stayed in America with my dad and I couldn't even communicate with him. Shortly after that, when I was nine, my father died. My mother was afraid I would grow up in a household primarily of women, so she involved me in athletics. My primary involvement was in shooting. That's where my friendships really began to be formed—and that's where the 'proxy' fathers come in. I became increasingly involved with this peer group of other shooters. I was the youngest, as a boy of sixteen, to shoot on the California five-man team.

"Just to be allowed to associate with the greatest shots in California, to be one of them, put me in a position to grow closer to them. It was a super relationship. These are the people who have remained friends all through my life, through the thick and thin of the motion-picture business. They have been a very important part of my life. My friendships with these men are more substantial than those I've made as a result of my acting career. I was much better known as a world-class shooter at the beginning of my career than as an actor. I am in the hall of fame for shooting and on the advisory board for Olympic shooting sports as well as for many other associations. I just went back to San Antonio for the world championships and I found that you *can* go home; my pictures are still up on the wall commemorating the time I broke the world record in the National Skeet Shooting Association competition. That part of my life is a constant that has carried me through all of the successes and failures that are inevitable for a performer.

"In the acting profession, with a few exceptions, an inherent competitive spirit inhibits close friendships. No matter how much you love somebody, if he takes a job from you it is very difficult to embrace that person and say 'Godspeed, old chap.' In the field of amateur sports it was different; survival wasn't at stake. In the world of motion pictures, friendships are largely transitory—once again, with a few exceptions—because they are based on direct survival, making a living. When I was a youngster my family knew Eddie Robinson. I played polo with Spencer Tracy. Gable and I used to go shooting together. But I was much younger than these people. Had we been closer in age, I would have been great friends with Spencer Tracy, Clark Gable, Gary Cooper and Bob Taylor. Our friendship would not have developed in the context of the motion-picture business but through duck shooting or polo playing. The catalytic agent would not have been show business. In fact, Gable never talked to me about show business until one night when he got crocked and I was up for an Academy Award. That's the only time he ever talked about show business.

"What happens in sports, in shooting, is that there are teams that work together with a firm loyalty. When we had team championships in shooting we were five men against the world, we held together. There was a cohesiveness, we were drawn together. Friendships are made from that type of situation—similar, on a smaller scale, to democracy. It works because people want it to work and must support it to make it work. I just finished the most expensive picture made this year: *1941.* The production company is called A Team, meaning that the entire group functions as a team. There are several of these teams in the company and they work together with a loyalty similar to the loyalty I found in athletics. This type of thing is important to friendship. It is, in my opinion, the real catalyst.

"In the motion picture business, the bottom line is survival—not success, not glory, but survival. The goal is to continue working, to be accepted. Since there are no rules, no specific system for who gets what part, the competition is fierce. That is why so many of our closest friendships, my wife's and mine, are not with show business people. Two of our closest friends are the caretakers up at our farm. For a lot of reasons—because we have fun together, because we shoot together, and because she works with my wife in fixing up the place—they are exciting and fun. He doesn't give a damn whether I end up being the world's greatest actor or fall on my ass.

"During the golden years, the years when there was more of a togetherness among actors, the years of Gable, Tracy, Cooper, and Bogey, there was a special kind of ambiance in the town. Those were more innocent times and friendship was easier to develop. Now, people are all over the place. Redford makes a film and goes back to Utah. DeNiro goes to New York. Everything is scattered. I think a communal interest of sorts is important for friendships. One of the reasons my wife and I get along so well is that we have, almost instinctively, similar reactions to situations. John Milius and I are friends. (He wrote *Apocalypse Now*, *Jeremiah Johnson*, and did *Judge Roy Bean*; he also produced *1941*, along with Spielberg.) He and I have a great common interest in clay-target sports, in the entire field. So, automatically, we are pulled together by an interest that is larger than either one of us. I find this very important; the friendship will find a strength because of our focus on something outside of ourselves. We don't just love each other for our individual qualities; that's a more hazardous kind of association.

"Crisis also draws people together. A friend is supposed to be there when needed; that's the point of friendship. Rock Hudson, for example, is a close friend for a lot of reasons that do not have to do with our business. He's absolutely unselfish. I was up for an Academy Award for a movie I made, *Written on the Wind*. At the time Rock had just done *Magnificent Obsession* and he was in very good shape at Universal, he was on top. I was on loan from Twentieth Century to Universal. Rock had plenty of clout at Universal and could have seen to it that I didn't get the flashiest part. No way! He didn't interfere. That's unusual. When my daughter was born, I was working on location. Rock had an

airplane fly by with a banner behind it which read, 'It's a girl.'
These are the moments that make friendships work. I don't see
Rock that often, but if he ever was in trouble I'd be there. And
he would be there for me. When my wife had a severe auto
accident, the caretaker of my farm was there—he was there for
thirty-six hours without sleep. That's where it's at. When the
chips are down, that's when friendship is tested."

JANE PAULEY, *NBC "Today Show"*

"I spot a friend when all the pretense is stripped away and I'm
not Jane Pauley, NBC, 'Today.' If I'm still comfortable and I feel
accepted, that's a friend. A friend is someone who laughs at my
jokes, someone who feels comfortable enough to call me when
he or she needs somebody. Maybe there are levels or tiers of
friendship: I like a lot of people and I enjoy a lot of people, but I
don't consider them all close friends. A close friend is something
very, very special. I'm careful about that. If, for example, I have a
suspicion that someone wants to get close to me because I represent 'Today,' they aren't in any danger of becoming a friend.
I'm happy that the really dear friends I have are the friends I
had long before network television. My friends have kept me
sane. If my celebrity consciousness gets out of hand they put
things into perspective. My sister, especially. She's my best friend.

"I have some very, very good friends but I've been moving so
much that circumstance has limited new friendships for the last
five years. First I moved from Indianapolis to Chicago, where I
was a total stranger. After a year I came to New York as a
stranger; I have been in New York for two and a half years now.
I've had to leave a lot of the friends I grew up with and went to
school with in Indianapolis. I suppose school friends tend to
scatter anyway, but the best friends I have now are still two or
three women from college. Recently I received a letter from one
of them who had been through some bad times and was coming
out of it. That kind of letter is physical evidence of the bond we

still share. And there are new friends who I think will become life-long friends. I have been increasingly aware in the last few years of my growing need to pay attention to and care for my friendships.

"Now that I am in a relationship, I am meeting new people. The best compliment I've received was at a party, a circle of friends of which I was the newest member, when two of the women acknowledged that I was a full-fledged member of the group. That was very meaningful. It's gratifying now to be accepted by his friends, but I continue to have my own. I remember my mother telling me when I was a child, 'When you get married you lose your friends and take his friends,' and I think she said that with a twinge of bitterness. That's something I wouldn't want to happen. One of my worst experiences was when a friend got married, moved away and suddenly we weren't friends anymore. We had grown up together, we were so close and then we weren't anything to each other. Not friends, not enemies, not anything. The breach was repaired, I can't remember quite how, and we are fast friends again. Only we are friends as adults now. It's quite different from being friends at fifteen. It's not the same type of friendship, we are different than we were at fifteen. We endorse each other as adults. As difficult as our parting was, there is something wonderful about the renewal and rediscovery of an old friend.

"Some of my newer friends are men. There are two that I'm pretty sure are going to be lifelong friends. We may not develop the intimacy that I expect from women friends, but if something good happens, I'm going to share it with them. I talked to both of them recently after a couple of rather interesting things had happened to me. They called to check in and to tease me a bit; it was wonderful making that kind of contact. Interestingly, the man in my life does not mind these male friendships. If anything, his example is encouraging because he takes care of his friendships as no one else I know. His dearest friends date back to school, but he has friends he met a year ago whom he calls, sends postcards to, has lunch with. He feels horrible if he lets a month go by without keeping in touch. I, on the other hand, succumb to my schedule and let friendships go for a while. Through his example, though, I realized that if I wasn't more attentive, one day I would want my friends and they wouldn't be there.

"I was once in the position of realizing a friend needed me a lot less than I needed her. That was very hurtful. Suddenly it became 'I don't have time, I'm going to a movie with so and so.' That was difficult, but otherwise I've been very fortunate in my friendships. I've been very fortunate in life. I haven't been through marriage, much less divorce. My family for the most part has been healthy. The things you turn to friends for—the life crises—haven't really occurred. A dear friend, however, found herself in a full-length cast with a small baby to care for. This happened while she was still struggling with the separation from her job and the feeling that the world was passing her by. And then the baby had what appeared to be a brain tumor. For a week in her life she agonized over that. When that crisis was over I got a letter—'Jane, he's going to be OK but as soon as I can get away, can I come visit?' You take so much from a friendship it was gratifying to be able to give."

EDWIN NEWMAN, *Newscaster and Author*
(Strictly Speaking, Sunday Punch)

"My experience with friendship has been made difficult by my travels and the fact that I was stationed in Europe for about twelve years. When you are overseas on assignment for as long as I was, you can't keep up with many people in this country. It began to be a chore for them as well as for me. It has been hard keeping up friendships, being away so much of the time; some have fallen by the wayside. My first job after World War II was in Washington; when I left Washington some good friends were left behind. I had friends from my college days, but they too tend to be scattered. And I have friends I made in the Navy who are also far away. So although I have several friends, many are geographically distant. I've found friends wherever I've been, but because I've been in so many places my friends are not necessarily surrounding me here at home. My wife has a similar experience. Many of her friends are in England—she's a British citizen. She has friends from her childhood, girls she went to school with, whom I've met, but the nature of things, the distance, makes it a difficult arrangement.

"The only friend I have now from my younger days is somebody I met in high school. I don't have any friends from my boyhood. Although the exposure of being on television, I've found, leads people that you may not have seen for years or even decades to get in touch with you. Only recently I have been in touch with two men from my boyhood—they contacted me and we had lunch together. It was very pleasant. In contrast, about seven or eight years ago a less pleasant and rather strange experience occurred with a man from my high school days. This is a fellow with whom I had been fairly friendly. He seemed to be very much down on his luck and when he spotted me in the street he said caustically, 'Well, you've done alright for yourself,' and he walked away. I hadn't seen him for thirty-five years, yet I remembered his name and called to him. He just continued down Fiftieth Street. I didn't know what to do; I had to make a plane and I had a bad leg at the time so I couldn't pursue him. I don't know what I would have done anyway if I had caught up with him. I would have tried to help. Although there's always a factor that could hold you back: Don't get involved. But I just never saw him again.

"There is a theory that it is very difficult to make close, lasting friendships when you are no longer young. I certainly don't avoid making friends, but the theory may apply to me. Early shared experiences, high school, college and the beginning days on the job tend to create lasting friendships. When you are older, meeting a new colleague may lead you to suggest, 'We ought to get together for dinner,' but probably you'll never get to it. I find that I don't particularly look for friends in my field, nor do I spend a great deal of time with others in this business. I don't know why, but it may some something to do with the fact that New York is a very big city. It might be different in Washington, which is considerably smaller, or overseas where English was not spoken and consequently English-speaking newspeople were drawn together. But in a city as large as New York, I only occasionally meet people from NBC, CBS or ABC, and I don't really seek them out. Occasionally, people from outside the business seek me out. However, this does not occur all that often. New York is a city where celebrities are somewhat taken in stride. If people stop you it is not to form a friendship but to chat, to comment on a program or a book; they want to say hello.

"When I think of my friendships it is very hard to pinpoint precisely how or when we decided to be friends. I don't know whether I've ever consciously thought about the qualities that I seek in a friend, but I suppose having some of the same assumptions is important. Otherwise, you'd waste a lot of time explaining before you get to the essence of your statement. There needs to be some understanding of each other, some mutual assumptions about the world. Obviously, there need to be some shared interests, similar attitudes. There is just some shared understanding that expresses itself in a desire to be with a person; there is a certain relaxation with each other. If you had to be on the alert all of the time, cautious with a person, it would not be much of a friendship. A friend is, most of all, someone with whom you don't have to pretend. Of course, a friend is someone you can count on. Fortunately, when I have called on friends it has not been a critical issue. For example, on one occasion when I was out of the country I had forgotten something that I needed. I called on an old friend to go to my apartment and get this thing and mail it to me in London. I feel I could turn to a friend for something more substantial, but I have not had to do that.

"I'd say that the friends I've kept—mostly outside of my work —are certainly not in awe of what I do—nor should they be.

They are perfectly successful on their own. Even if they weren't, though, they would understand that being in television is only a way of making a living. In that sense it is similar to other means of employment. My friends don't ask me very much about my work most of the time. . . . I like the way my wife thinks of friendship. To her, a real friend is someone you would be willing to have stay in your home or with whom you would stay. When you imagine being with someone for a period, being that close, it is a good indication of friendship. To call somebody a friend, you really have to want to be with that person. To wake up in the morning and be pleased that they are there—that's a friend."

DICK CLARK, *Entertainer/Producer*

"I have very few close friends and those that I am close with I don't see very often. I live such a terribly hectic life and, since a good friendship needs nurturing and time, my circle of close friends is necessarily small. Even with friends I feel close to—lifelong friends for that matter—it is difficult to get together. I am about to ask a favor of a friend that I've had for over twenty years. I don't think we've seen each other more than a dozen times in as many years. But we write, we phone back and forth, we send 'obscene' letters to each other and do all sorts of dumb things that reinforce the friendship. Right now I need a big favor from him. I expect that he'll rise to the occasion; I know I can count on him unless it's just physically impossible for him to help me.

"The true test of friendship in my peculiar occupation—working all hours of the day and night all over the world—is a relationship that stays alive without an awful lot of contact. My wife and I have a favorite couple we call to join us whenever we have a special occasion. They are in the same business—she is an actress and he is a television performer—and are also very busy working much of the time. If they are unavailable, we have to understand. Even if the occasion is important we can't get hurt feelings because they are unable to join in our celebration. We may even have to celebrate an occasion, perhaps an anniversary or a birthday, on a different date, one that's convenient to our friends. Those kinds of accommodations are essential if I am going to maintain a friendship in my world. To a person in my business it is important to do what is necessary to hold onto good friends because time demands make it difficult to develop new friendships.

"In addition to a few close friends I have a varied and wide circle of people I am fond of and consider to be friends. My wife and I are best friends. We work together and are true friends. There are also many business associates I see frequently and whose company I enjoy. Some of the better friends that I have developed over the years are in the entertainment business. I am also close to others who are my arch competitors—we compete very strongly in the same arena. Since we are successful it is not much of a problem—we know we'll win one, lose one, but still maintain a viable enterprise. If I beat them out of ten deals in a row that would probably disrupt the relationship. The likelihood of the balance tipping so drastically, though, is very small.

"I don't currently have a neighborhood friend. I know my neighbors and we are friendly; if there were an emergency, if the house was on fire, we'd be there for each other. I'd leave the keys with them and all that sort of thing. But it's not really a friendship, it's more a cooperative neighborly relationship. At one point in my life, though, one of the best friends I had was a neighbor. He was a physician living across the street when I lived in Philadelphia. But life in Philadelphia is a lot different from life in California. Philadelphia still has the concept of the old traditional neighborhood. This man, my neighbor and friend, was there through the difficulties of my former marriages—he saw me at my best and at my worst. We had a very close relationship but we haven't seen each other in years.

"Another friend I turned to for help and advice during the time of my unhappy marriages was an entertainer who has subsequently died. His assistance was important to be because he was not emotionally entangled in the situation and he was honest. He bolstered my spirits and helped clarify my thoughts. I appreciated that because very early in my life I was hurt by friendship. As a kid in my twenties I was used by friends. Of course, some of my friends were very sincere people. But others were rapists. By that I mean they were deceitful, they took advantage and betrayed my trust. As a result I became wary of friendship for a while. To some extent those experiences have influenced me to be a rather private, reserved person. To some I may even appear cold.

"I have found that people of very modest means and the very rich make very good friends because they don't want anything from you. People of very modest income often have the same philosophy of life as very wealthy people—'whatever I have is yours.' It's very interesting. I have known many such people and they have always shared their home, their food and even whatever money they had. The wealthy may do the same in a slightly different way because they too are not looking to get anything back. The people in the middle, the climbers, make the worst friends because they always have angles.

"I have, unfortunately, lost some friends to success, but I feel it's mostly because of the propaganda that people hear about how fame changes people. Actually I don't think celebrity status changes people. It is more likely that people simply react to celebrities differently. Often it is those people around the celebrity who change. I've heard it again and again from people in the public eye that all kinds of rumors are spread about them and as a result they are treated differently. Most of the gossip is pure nonsense but occasionally it can, if taken seriously, cause a split in a friendship."

Unlike other people interviewed about their friendship experiences, celebrities didn't have the benefit of anonymity nor did they comprise a balanced sample. There were several refusals, and many celebrities simply didn't reply to my invitation. Of those who consented to discuss their friendships, contrivance, of course, is always a possibility, but lack of candor is usually apparent—particularly to a veteran interviewer. This occurred on one occasion and the celebrity interview was discarded—as were a handful of interviews—when I felt a survey respondent to be unusually evasive or untruthful. For the most part, the celebrities interviewed spoke freely and there is no reason to believe their statements to be mere extensions of their "public image."

Just as the more formal survey data yield valuable information, the celebrity interviews are also enlightening. Over and over, the sentiments of all of us—our friendship desires, our disappointments and excitements—were echoed. The issues of success, competition, loyalty and conflict were similar to those we all face with our friends. Perhaps more so than most of us, celebrities are aware of being used but none seemed overly wary. Is it lonelier at the top? Do the famous lack friends? Although a reliable answer could only be obtained with a large-scale investigation, the responses gathered here do not support the popular contention of friendlessness. If anything, celebrities appeared to regard their friendship networks more highly than the rest of us.

Making Friendship Work:
Key Ingredients

Remedying Emotional Deficiency

EDWARD ELLIS, a forty-four-year-old journalist, is gregarious, charming and quite likable. Yet, despite having a large social circle and engaging in as many activities as possible, he often felt out of sorts. To his many acquaintances he seemed busy, active and involved in the world; the lump he felt in the pit of his stomach, the emptiness he experienced practically all the time, was not apparent to outsiders. Through physical activity and tranquilizers, Mr. Ellis attempted to rid himself of this mysterious, unpleasant feeling. Finally, after a thorough medical examination which revealed him to be in good health, his physician stated that his symptoms were similar to those of depression. Out of desperation he followed his physician's advice and consulted with a psychologist. Now, three months after a year-long psychotherapy experience, Edward Ellis discusses the feelings that mystified him.

"At first the idea of psychological help seemed strange to me. I wondered, 'How can this help me—just talking about things that aren't even clear to me?' But I found that talking, having to put my vague thoughts into words, forced me to think of things I hadn't considered in many years; it had the effect of making me dig deep inside myself and bring up things I hardly knew were troubling me. As we continued to meet I spoke more easily of my relationships with other people. In one conversation I felt as if I had come to the edge of an awful canyon; I referred to it later as a pit I had dug for myself. I became aware that all these years were spent avoiding involvement with other people. I really had no close friends; there wasn't another person on this planet whose life would be affected if I disappeared. If someone was getting too close I limited the amount of time I spent with him; even if I revealed a personal feeling, I did so in a controlled manner, arranging not to see the person again for several weeks after that. That was my pattern—avoiding emotional intimacy or seeking it in very limited doses. When the cover is removed and my activity is slowed, it is painfully clear what I feel—lonely. At one point in our conversation I remarked that no one cares about me and I haven't let myself care about anyone. The statement was true and it was agonizing, but there was still a buffer between the words and my experience. It wasn't quite real, it didn't quite penetrate my armor. The therapist asked me to repeat my statement slowly and as I did so to focus on my feelings. I did it once and I started to feel weak; I felt wobbly even though I was seated. He asked me to do it again and I tried but I could barely speak. I felt more deeply disturbed than I can describe; I had reached a point far away from anything I had ever known. Despair, fear and grief—all greater than any I had felt before—were evoked by my loneliness. Suddenly I was engulfed in emotion beyond anything I had ever experienced.

"As soon as the session ended I went home and forced myself

to sleep. I was scared and unhappy when I woke up. I couldn't rid myself of the thought that I had withdrawn from significant human contacts; I was not even intimate with myself. I would not allow myself to experience my feelings about myself and I managed to avoid the intensity of the previous conversation. I was angry and confused, afraid of what I felt and even more frightened of what I might say or do next. I felt lost and for the first time since childhood I felt real panic. I skipped several appointments in an effort to run away from what I was feeling, but I found it impossible to deny. The therapist encouraged me gently but persistently to risk being open, to let things happen to my feelings and to expose them. Eventually, somewhat calmed, I dared to return to this issue of my loneliness. I spoke of my deep-seated conviction that other people cannot be trusted, that it is terribly dangerous to open oneself up to them. I recalled reaching out to my parents—especially my father—only to be rebuffed; when I made tentative, affective overtures to other important persons in my life, I got clobbered. On the basis of these hurtful experiences I had adopted the tactic of self-alienation. The fact that I had socialized a lot meant nothing; one way or another I let it be known that the relationship stopped where intimacy began. There were always reservations. I always protected myself from being exposed—from being hurt. My friendships, without exception, were counterfeit. The lump in my stomach and my depression were body messages telling me I was emotionally starving despite all the outward appearances to the contrary."

In contrast to the more casual interactions between social acquaintances, friendship relations are characterized by keen interest in the subjective and personal side of another individual. To have a personal involvement with a friend means to be interested in his or her well-being, his or her unique identity and perceptions of the world. As more is learned about the conditions of psychological health, the suspicion grows stronger that inability to enter into and sustain such personal relations with others results in the emergence of disturbing symptoms. Investigating the emotional factors in everything from minor backache to cancer, the psychology of interpersonal relations is increasing in importance. As Edward Ellis realized, the desire for human intimacy cannot be ignored; it is necessary for healthy functioning.

Indisputably, friendship can potentially provide the psychological nutrients so important for optimal, zestful living. However, as with all interpersonal relationships, friendship is also potentially harmful. Thus, as in teacher-student, parent-child or doctor-patient relationships, the consequences may be constructive or deteriorative. Consider the myth that students need only have intellectually resourceful and knowledgeable teachers to grow intellectually. When the data are examined it is found that teachers who provide a sound emotional relationship with children elicit as much as five times the achievement growth over the course of a year as those who coldly pursue intellectual development. Documentation of similar relationship issues—most notably the psychotherapy relationship—is growing. The direct implication is that the quality of an interpersonal relationship may retard or advance an individual's psychological development.

When one is involved in a prolonged, ongoing relationship with persons having certain characteristics, the chances of impaired functioning—physical or emotional—are increased. Being obliged to remain in close contact with someone on whom we are dependent, for instance, can, if this person is obnoxious and overdemanding, literally give rise to a "pain in the neck," headache, digestive upsets and other psychosomatic maladies. The experience of those in the psychological professions has amply demonstrated that the relationship of parents to their children—especially when parents make excessive or contradictory demands on their children—can be an influencing factor in the development of neurotic or psychotic symptoms.

Some of us have found our sense of well-being promoted by our interpersonal relationships. As a result of a friendship some people have been influenced not only to think differently about superficial matters but to transform their attitudes about life profoundly. In one investigation, improvement was greater on several psychological indices when a troubled individual consulted with a motivated friend who understood him, as opposed to a professional psychotherapist. There is even some evidence that appearance can change, that physical health is improved by some relationships. Many physicians who have become alert to interpersonal sources of stress have been able to prove that for given patients, their symptoms of asthma, skin eruptions, hypertension and other physical symptoms disappeared with the development of more satisfying relationships.

Given the importance of a relationship's quality, a crucial question is prompted: *What are the characteristics of friendships which are compatible with psychological health, and what are the characteristics of friendships which undermine healthy functioning?* With vague standards we all offer our own judgments. "He has a beautiful relationship with his friend"; "she and her husband have a sick relationship"; "their friendship won't last." Aside from being vague, these are judgments based on personal bias; they do not necessarily enlighten us as to universal standards. In this chapter the professional literature gathered over the last decade has been consulted in an effort to answer the question posed above. That is, dimensions of healthy human relationships as well as those factors which decay and adversely affect individuals will be considered.

Nutrients

A good deal of the stress and the strain of the human condition comes from our striving to be something that we are not. Related to this is our failure to accept ourselves and others as is. Two of the nutrients to be discussed focus specifically on these issues: authenticity and acceptance. The third dimension found to be important for fostering and maintaining high-quality friendships is the ability to communicate effectively and make our wants and expectations known. To the extent that these factors in combination exist at high levels, the friendship participants are likely to thrive.

The Courage to Be: Authenticity. While most of us want a close friendship, we also fear that in the process of meeting someone and becoming known to this person we may be found undesirable. For some people, this fear of rejection results in the formation of a false front, a mask to avoid being known. Hidden behind this mask is usually the belief, conscious or implicit, that to be one's real self is dangerous, that exposure of real feeling will lead to being unwanted: "If people found out what I was really like, they wouldn't want any part of me." One woman who felt this way described her dilemma, how confused and empty she had become regarding her own convictions:

"During grade school, I had fantasies of being accepted by girls I admired, but I never approached them. I selected my friends from those who approached me. In high school I was considered shy; I was aware of those people I really wanted to know yet I would form friendships with people who were not my first choice. Now I am more selective but I still play it safe and cautious. I still experience a tension when I'm with other people. I'm more relaxed by myself. I realized recently that when I'm alone I don't have to perform; this accounts for the reduction in tension. Over the years I have developed a knack for determining what kind of individual the other person likes and then pretending to be that individual. Even if this puts my companions at ease it creates a tension within me; since they have an inaccurate concept of me, I am left with the burden of maintaining the phoniness.

"When I'm in a social situation, a party for instance, I could be lively and appear to be having a good time but all the while I'd be putting on a little drama, creating the illusion that I'm bright and interesting so that other people will see me as attractive. I am always aware of being judged; it is very important for me to gain the approval of someone I admire. Sometimes I even surprise myself by taking positions that I don't really feel if I think that would please somebody I want to impress. It's been so long since I stood up for my convictions that I don't know what I feel or what my convictions really are. I haven't been honestly myself. I don't know what my real self is; I've lost touch with my inner experience.

"One of the few times that I allowed myself to be off guard, I couldn't handle it. I was involved in a group discussion and my face was flushed, my tone communicated anger, I was shaking my finger at this other woman. Yet when one of the other people said, 'Well, let's not get angry about this,' I replied with sincerity and surprise, 'I'm not angry! I don't have any feeling about this at all! I was just pointing out the logical facts.' The other people in the group, seeing my obvious anger, broke out in laughter at my statement and I was utterly embarrassed. My defensiveness, my unwillingness to be myself kept me from being aware of my anger at the moment. I realize now I was terribly angry at that other woman, even though at the time I thought I wasn't."

This woman is beginning to discover that her behavior and even the feelings she experiences do not flow naturally from her genuine reactions, but are a façade behind which she has been hiding. She is discovering how much of her life is guided by what she thinks she should be rather than by what she is. Still more disturbing, she recognizes that she exists in response to the demands of others, that she seems to have no direction of her own.

Frequently, when people relate in an inauthentic, contrived manner there are signals to this effect. An atmosphere of strain, artificiality, anxiety and tension prevails. With such an individual we often sense that what is being said is almost certainly a front, a cover-up for the fear that they are unworthy as they are. We wonder what he or she *really* feels or thinks. We wonder if *they* know what they feel. We tend to be wary and cautious with such an individual. The contact leaves one feeling empty, it is not nourishing.

It is only natural to want to be liked and appreciated by other people, but being unnatural in order to accomplish this ultimately inhibits closeness and results in self-alienation. Those who are stuck in this behavior, not occasionally, but as a continuing, repetitive pattern, may socialize, meet many people and even boast of a wide circle of friends, but essentially they remain unrevealed, and hence unconnected; inauthenticity and lasting friendships do not mix.

In contrast to contrivance, authentic interpersonal behavior is not effortful, planned or deliberately assumed. Rather, it is spontaneous and unpremeditated. Such behavior, in the long run, turns out to be flexible and versatile; the contact feels good, it is fulfilling. To pick an easily recognized example, consider the infant. If an infant expresses affection or anger or contentment or fear there is no doubt in our minds that he or she *is* the experience, all the way through. The infant is transparently fearful or loving or angry or whatever, there is no deception. Perhaps that genuineness is why so many people respond warmly to infants—we feel we know exactly where we stand with them.

What Is, Is: Acceptance. Many of us are unaware of the tremendous pressure we put on mates, children and friends to have the same feelings we do. It is often as though we silently say, "If you want me to like you, then you must feel as I do. If I feel your behavior is bad, you must feel so too. If I feel a certain goal is desirable, you must feel so too." A healthy interpersonal relationship precludes the demand that "you must think, feel and act like me." It is characterized by respect and acceptance of a friend as a separate, unique person without demanding that he or she be otherwise. To respect and value another's individuality includes not only those characteristics that are considered socially desirable, but also traits that might be called faults.

Just as authenticity—being freely and deeply oneself without façades—is important to friendship, being able to express the various facets of our personality without the fear of harsh judgment is also of significant value. A sound friendship permits the expression of anger, childishness and silliness as well as affection, since if there is no danger that we will be condemned if we drop our front, we can be as we really are, weak when we feel weak, scared when we feel confused, childish when the responsibilities of adulthood are looming too heavy.

What does the experience of acceptance feel like? Keith, a forty-eight-year-old high school English teacher, was divorced three months when he met Helen, a woman with whom he developed a stormy but beneficial relationship. Keith has a warm, pleasant face and his eyes become misty as he discusses this aspect of his friendship with Helen.

"When I met Helen one of my strongest and most persistent feelings was pain—not just emotional pain but actual physical pain, nausea, headaches and the like. I remember saying once that when my wife left me for another man and I lost the connection to my family, it was as if a knife was put into me and was being turned around each day to cut up my insides. My first reaction to Helen was one of surprise at her sensitivity and awareness of what and how I was feeling, even when I expressed it inarticulately or hardly at all. Then I began to get the feeling that not only was she sensitive but she also cared about me. It seems crazy but I fought desperately against this feeling. I was firmly convinced that to give in to her acceptance of me meant to sell my soul; there was a high price for allowing another person into my life. Indeed, I was still reeling from the last time I yielded.

"I tried demonstrating to her how unworthy I was—how selfish, inadequate, nasty. I tried hating and attacking her. I told her that she couldn't possibly think well of me, that I was defective. I suspected that she was being deceitful and cruel in pretending that she accepted me. But she was always there, treating me with respect; she was a firm, strong pillar which I beat on to no avail and which merely said, 'You are a worthwhile human being.' She saw past my bullshit yet she didn't condemn me for it. Not that she was a saint; she expressed anger, outrage and frustration. She engaged me and fought ferociously, but she always did so in a way which didn't belittle me. Her words were strong yet soft; somehow the sharp edges were removed. She conveyed that I was a person acting in an obnoxious manner, I was not an obnoxious person. In other words, I was not disqualified and considered garbage because of my foibles.

"As I look at it now, I was putting all my faults and felt inadequacies on the line so that I could be done with the process of rejection. And Helen calmly (and sometimes not so calmly), by her acceptance of me as a person, peeled off layer after layer of my armor. Slowly, it became clear that it was safe; I realized that I am the one who makes the ultimate judgment of my worth. That sounds like a simple, common-sense statement. Yet, my appreciation of that dictum has given me such a sense of peace that it is awesome. I feel elevated, freer, not only more accepting of myself but also of others. In my relationships with other people, I try to see them as individuals struggling with the same things as I do, not as adversaries or enemies. Most of us want the same things in our relationships: honesty, a sharing of feelings and thoughts, empathy, support, fun. Keeping these things in mind, my tolerance has expanded and my friendships, as a result, are much richer."

It should not be construed from the foregoing that acceptance is the same thing as liking. Obviously, we may not like all that another person is, but by acceptance we acknowledge and respect the fact that he or she is still worthwhile; it is the attitude that expresses: I may not like such and such about you but that doesn't make you less of a person. The people with this characteristic tend to be flexible and adaptable to change, and accepting of other people even when they disagree with them. They are trusting of themselves and humankind and optimistic in their outlook on life.

The feeling of being accepted is not something we can get from trees, mountains or even pets. It is only in our human relationships that this quality can be offered. It is found in varying degrees among good friends, mature lovers, wise parents and their children as well as between some educators and their students. And, it is precisely this feeling of being valued that promotes our fullest functioning with other people.

Please, Tell Me What You Want: Direct Expression. "We're not communicating" is the classic complaint in many relationships. Actually, in relating to another person it is impossible *not* to communicate. Words can be used to hurt, calm, nurture, confuse, anger, provoke, deceive, dominate, manipulate—the list is endless. Even silence conveys a message. The ways one behaves, moves, gestures all transmit messages. Problems arise when the messages we send are not the messages received. This is always a risk in relationships—that we will be misunderstood—but it is particularly common when indirectness and subtlety are relied on heavily. When words are used to camouflage, when messages are hidden and indirect, they usually introduce further confusion into a situation that is often already difficult.

"When did you get back in town?" may appear to be an innocent request for information. But if the questioner already knows that his friend has been home for a week and is angry that he hasn't been called, then the question is not so innocent; it is an indirect, vague expression of a feeling: "I know you've been home for a week and I'm angry that you didn't call"; or, "I want you to show me that you care by calling and I'm hurt that you didn't." As it stood, the intent of the question was manipulative; if the response was honest it gives the angry friend "permission" to show his anger, and if the response was a lie it offers the opportunity for the manipulator to begin a game of "I gotcha."

One area where indirectness and manipulation occur with great frequency is in making requests. Many of us do not want to take responsibility for what we want so we speak in generalities, cajole, offer "innocent" suggestions, question and accuse. Behind these tactics is the attitude: "I expect you to satisfy my desires without having to ask you so that I do not run the risk of appearing needy, feeling foolish or being rejected."

It is a sunny Saturday in August and Steven is preparing to go to the beach to meet his friend Daryl when Jerry calls.

Steven: Hi, Jerry. How are you?

Jerry: Fine. I've been pretty busy at work. Everything there is as chaotic as usual.

Steven: Sounds similar to my place, it's a nuthouse. Listen, I've got to get going, I'm meeting Daryl at the beach and I'm already running late. I'll get back to you tonight.

Jerry: (Feeling hurt at not being invited) Gee, I haven't been to the beach in weeks. Perfect weather for it today.

Steven: Yeah, I'm really looking forward to getting away from it all for the day.

Jerry: (Continuing to bait an invitation) You know, I haven't seen Daryl in ages. How's he doing?

Steven: (Becoming impatient) Fine, fine, listen. . . .

Jerry: (Persistently, with a trace of annoyance in his voice) I was wondering, Steve, maybe we can get together sometime?

Ideally, Steven might have invited Jerry along. But to expect that other people will always be pleasant and act in our best interest is unrealistic—people do not take their cues from our silent hopes. If it hurts not being invited, it hurts more to conceal the wound. In short, requests ("Can I come along?") which are unspoken are frequently disastrous. If one doesn't know what's wanted of him or her it's difficult for the person to fulfill the request or understand the emotions the other person experiences in disappointment. In most of these instances both individuals are likely to draw apart. If one is manipulated by tone or by carefully chosen words he or she usually feels uneasy—vaguely guilty and confused—and the manipulator, especially if unsuccessful, will probably feel cheated. As the rancor created by indirectness escalates, it mushrooms into other areas of the relationship. That is, once a negative destructive atmosphere of misunderstanding is established, more indirectness and misunderstanding are likely to follow as protection against the "enemy."

An individual such as Jerry may begin to attack Steven on any number of insignificant issues—his dress, a mannerism, his habits and so on. In actuality, Jerry's disturbance is related to something entirely different—he feels left out, his feelings are hurt. If not brought out in the open, these kinds of feelings often end in an argument, the source of which is unclear or disguised; the result after many futile bouts is frequently of the you-hurt-me-so-I'll-hurt-you-variety. In many instances vindictiveness becomes the major force in the gradual weakening of the relationship.

There is no guaranteed way to avoid misunderstandings with a friend, but one thing is sure—coaxing, cajoling, dropping "cute" hints, manipulating and beating around the bush are all barriers to clear communications. When something is wanted, be it change, clarification, reassurance, companionship or support, it is important that the message be direct and to the point. Speaking in generalities won't get the job done.

When people know what they want from each other, they have established clear communication and contact; they are in a position to attempt an agreement regarding their desires. They may discover that some desires ("always be there when I need you") can't possibly be satisfied, other desires may meet with an unwillingness, and still others will be satisfied. Possibly, by being open about what they want, two individuals may realize that they are too different to get along and that they would be less frustrated if their relationship were more casual. Whatever solution is arrived at is certain to be preferable to the endless struggle and tense undercurrent that results from continuing to demand what someone is not able or is unwilling to provide.

Toxins

Just as the dimensions of authenticity, acceptance and direct expression facilitate healthy functioning, others destroy it. There are two major friendship toxins. The first, a vicious and vindictive characteristic, is blame. The other is a form of clinging and demanding dependency that controls individuals not so much by overpowering them as by bleeding the life out of them. In either case, whether through constant blaming or clinging dependency, these characteristics wear people down; they inhibit real intimacy. We get involved with the "blamer" or "clinger" at considerable peril.

It's All Your Fault: Blame. Two friends have a falling out. It begins because one of them, Stacy, feels irritated with the other, Joan, about some minor issue. They part that evening without saying a word to each other. The next day Stacy is no longer angry at Joan and would like to have contact with her, talk to her, be friendly once again. Joan, not knowing that Stacy's anger has passed and fearing that she is still upset, decides to wait until she gets some indication that Stacy is ready to act more kindly. Stacy, although calmed down, still views the spat as Joan's fault and is not willing to reach out and make contact herself, although she would be receptive to Joan's initiative. At work the next day she begins to blame Joan for not making a move—for not doing something she herself is unwilling to do.

A man feels ill at ease going to a theater, restaurant or any public place alone. Rather than struggling to overcome this, he asks a friend whom he has on occasion accommodated, to accompany him to the movies. His friend declines, suggesting he would meet him for dinner after the movie. He responds with, "Why are you so selfish?" and refuses the offer to have dinner together.

Tom, a young physician, is an extremely shy and self-effacing man. At a cocktail party he and his wife, a nurse, attended, the guests sat around the periphery of a large banquet room. Drinks and hors d'oeuvres were placed on a table in the center of the room and guests—mostly Tom's hospital colleagues—helped themselves as they desired. Tom, however, feeling too self-conscious to get up and walk to the center of the room, remained seated, hungry and disgruntled. His wife, neither hungry nor thirsty, was engrossed in conversation with another nurse. On the way home Tom was silent and sullen. After continued prodding, he angrily declared, "You and your low-brow friends—at least they could serve some decent food!"

In all the above examples, the blamer has the attitude, "I'm not responsible, you are." From this follows: "If you are responsible for my (our) discomfort, distress or unhappiness, only you can alter it. If only you would change, my problems would be solved." The characteristic exchange of those entangled in the blame-counterblame trap comes down to this: "It was your fault"; "no, it was yours." The result of this position is a preoccupation with mutual recrimination in which, at the very least, one or both friends are consistently hurt and conflicts are hardly ever resolved. Typically, the exchange of invectives is intended to reduce the friend's capacity to hurt; each tries through fault-finding to deflate the other. And so one friend may dredge up the past, using yesterday's failures as today's ammunition, while the other retaliates by injuring him in the same way. Each focuses on the other's frailties illegitimately; the effort is not directed toward understanding but toward destroying or demeaning an "opponent."

Aside from shifting responsibility, blame is used as a way of avoiding self-examination. Some people, for example, counter all criticism by blaming the person who is criticizing them. If a man or woman prone to this is accused of being dishonest in a particular situation, he or she might counter with "Well, you're dishonest too." If he or she is accused of being inconsiderate, it is "You have been inconsiderate also." If someone expresses resentment, the response might be, "There are a number of things I resent about you, too." In all instances defending rather than listening is the result.

In another blame-related tactic intended to serve the same purpose—disarm any and all criticism—some individuals do just the opposite: They suggest that they are among the very worst of people, that they hardly have a redeeming feature. People who put themselves down, who turn blame on themselves, are often saying, "Don't bother criticizing me. I have already attacked my-self and done a better, harsher job of it than you possibly could."

Regardless of the manner in which blame (you are one hundred percent wrong and I'm one hundred percent right) is used, the inevitable effect is to pull people apart. Indeed, when friendships are steeped in blaming behavior, at least one of the friends is often using the maneuver in order to justify keeping the relationship distant. They may no longer bear the other person any positive feelings yet are too insecure to say so clearly and go their separate ways.

The antithesis of blame and defensiveness is to assume responsibility for one's own feelings, openly look at what part one plays in an unhappy circumstance, and avoid repeating that role in the future. For example, if a man can admit he is afraid that he is failing at his job instead of attacking his friend for his success, support and helpfulness are possible. Tolerance and generosity become easier when an individual openly acknowledges his fallibility. Similarly, if a person is courageous and honest enough to admit his mistake—and finds he is forgiven—it then becomes possible for him to be tolerant of his friends' foibles. One thing is certain: Blame and the resultant refusal to take adult responsibility for oneself are potent enough to contaminate the entire spectrum of friendship behavior.

The Clinging Vine: Excessive Dependency. All human beings are dependent. As children we are dependent on adults for our existence; a newborn infant is among the most helpless of living organisms. For sheer survival, the infant needs other people—parents or parent surrogates—to behave in ways which will bring need satisfaction. The parent must provide food and arrange the environment so that the child will stay alive, relatively free from pain and able to grow. As the child develops physically, so that he or she becomes more capable of learning, other people are needed as models to emulate. The child needs to hear people talk, for example, so that he or she can learn to talk. He or she needs, in the early days of life, a lot of contact—caressing, holding and social stimulation; there is evidence that without such close contact, the child's physical and psychological development will be impaired.

As adults we are dependent on others for the exchange of goods and services as well as companionship and emotional gratification. We are, by nature, communal and we rely on our ability to communicate and relate to our fellows. Experimental isolation studies demonstrate that long periods of seclusion from other living creatures tend to produce hallucinations and other pathological symptoms. It seems that just as tissues need oxygen, our psychic processes require contact and involvement with other people. This is not to say that periods of separation from others are dangerous to one's well-being; indeed there is evidence that the healthiest personalities need and actively seek solitude in order to contemplate and to discover their authentic feelings and beliefs.

While dependency is a healthy and natural part of the life process, it can be corrupted, it can become excessive. We all know this, but some of us find it difficult to accept—especially when we want a particular friend to be with us. This refusal to accept another person as an individual free to see other friends or to pursue independent interests will reflect poorly on friendship.

Dysfunctional, relationship-eroding dependency is found among people who have lost touch with their values and their strength. Consequently, they need other people to lean on, to provide them with a sense of wholeness and to reassure them by means of approval, that they can function. It is as if self-esteem is not contained within the person but has been passed on to the judgment of others. This kind of person will often feel unable to tolerate being alone since being in his or her own company feels like being in the company of nobody. They will pass countless evenings on meaningless social gatherings, will have endless and pointless conversations with people (the actual point being to hold the listener next to them so that they needn't stand alone) and will stay up far too late at parties—simply to avoid being alone.

In the dependent friendship, growth and development are stifled rather than enhanced. The relationship is overworked, overloaded, and there is an insistence that an undue degree of emotional support be provided. Often one party in the relationship begins pulling the other down, and a negative cycle is the result: Each one's negative qualities or attitudes feed the other's back and forth in a diminishing spiral that can destroy the relationship.

One such destructive friendship involved David and Sid, two twenty-five-year-old men who were inseparable. They worked together in an electronics firm, usually took their vacations together and often double dated. David was content with his life, but Sid was growing and wanted more for himself than his present job provided. He considered going back to school for an engineering degree. David, threatened by Sid's ambitions and the possible loss of the relationship, attempted discouraging him: "How could you work all day and study at night? Why bother? Engineers don't have job security anyway" were typical undermining remarks. After a while, Sid began to feel "sucked dry" and "emptied" by David's complaints and his neediness. Moreover, he strongly resented David's attempts to undermine his confidence. David's tactics to lower Sid's esteem and thus continue the old pattern of being able to cling to him for security only succeeded in pushing him away.

We do need emotional closeness, we do need to know someone cares for us, we do have a need for close, interdependent friendships and we also need to grow. But we cannot grow in dependent relations of the type being discussed. Our friendships can only be vital and sustained to the extent that they tap and encourage the actualization of our own courage and strength, each of us receiving from others the support necessary to our growth and giving back to others the support they need for their growth.

Assessing Your Friendships

Most of us bring both nourishing and toxic qualities to our friendships. The objective is one of maximizing the nourishing and minimizing the toxic. Perfection in this task is unlikely. However, through increasing our awareness of unhealthy (toxic) patterns and a willingness to replace them with new, healthier (nourishing) attitudes and behavior we can gradually improve our friendships.

Honest, persistent questioning is one method by which to enlighten ourselves. Consider the following issues: To what extent have the failures in my friendships been rooted in a fear of becoming vulnerable? Do I create friction in my friendships precisely because I am afraid of the risk taking and the self-revelation in the relationship? Is my relating largely perfunctory and void of expression of real feeling? Do I treat a friend poorly because I myself do not feel worthy? Do I feel an incompleteness concerning my own identity and look to my friends to fill this lack within myself? Have I turned a friend into a parent surrogate on whom I can take out my frustrations? Do I strive to promote growth in my friends? How much time and energy am I investing in allotting blame for conflicts and tensions that arise in my friendships? Do I resist manipulating my friends into satisfying my needs? How much time do I spend talking to others about a friend's faults, trying to win confirmation and support from them in my battle against him or her? Do I express appreciation and open affection to my friends?

An individual can ask himself questions like these, or two friends may engage in a dialogue based on these or similar questions in an effort to strengthen their friendship. Of course, immediate insightful answers will not always be forthcoming. An individual or two friends may well come up with few, if any, clear answers, or "answers" may be discovered that later prove to be false.

Honest scrutiny of actions and feelings is not a foolproof course. It is impossible to be sure whether one's inquiries are logical or self-deceptive, or to predict with complete accuracy the motivations underlying one's actions. But when your friendship, you well-being or your friend's well-being is at stake, this questioning process can be critical and instructive.

Along with questioning ourselves, we can gauge the quality of our friendships by how the contact feels. A nourishing friendship leaves us feeling energized and enriched. In contrast, a toxic contact, as with any poison, leaves us feeling tense, irritable and drained.

Protecting Friendship: A Potpourri of Suggestions

Each of us has a unique way of responding to life—a mosaic of our expectations, our hopes, our reality and our imagination. Friendship, a process which, by its very intimate nature, highlights our complexity, can be distracting, wearying and frustrating. Friendship makes life more complicated, but there is no other way to be fully human. Sometimes, with our emphasis on self-development and individual freedom, we lose sight of that basic emotional fact. And so, whether we like it or not, if we want to promote our humanness, we must allow at least one other person to enter our life. Doing that isn't easy; and to expect continuous and perfect harmony in such a relationship is unrealistic. It is possible, however, to achieve a reasonably satisfying friendship by protecting it from unnecessary strain.

Friendship is strained when we become blind and insensitive to the feelings of our friends. The opposite of this "I don't care about your feelings" attitude is empathic communication. Empathy is an effort to understand another's beliefs, practices and feelings without necessarily sharing or agreeing with them. Empathy is made up of two main factors. One is listening and attempting to understand another's view rather than busily preparing a rebuttal. It is as if the listener were silently asking, "How does he (she) see it; how does he (she) feel; how would I feel if this were said to me?" The second aspect of empathy is communicating this understanding to the speaker.

A brief exercise that can help to develop this pattern of communicating is "role reversal." In this exercise, when a discussion involving personal/emotional issues occurs, it becomes the responsibility of each individual to state the other's position and feelings until he or she is satisfied with the degree of understanding. If he or she is not satisfied with the level of understanding, a brief "time out" is called while the position and related feelings are expressed again. The discussion does not proceed until each person is satisfied that the salient aspects of his or her positions are understood. For example:

George: I'm out there all day long, getting one turndown after another. Being a salesman is tough. Some days it really gets to me.

Peter: Hey, sitting in an office all day is no picnic either. What the hell are you complaining about?

George: Hold it. Time out! You passed right over my feelings. Can you please restate what I said from my viewpoint. (George is asking for an empathic response.)

Peter: It sounded as if you were about to call off our plans this weekend because you're beat and I don't want to hear about it. (Rather than being sensitive to George's feelings, Peter is still focusing on his own.)

George: That wasn't my intention. I was just feeling a bit discouraged and it's not that easy for me to admit that. Do you understand? (George is restating his position and asking Peter to express his understanding in his own words.)

Peter: I understand now. You are feeling frustrated after a day of rejection and, when you admitted that, *I* added to your feeling of rejection. It's just that I had a difficult day also and I thought I was about to get a rejection from you.

George: Sounds like you're also pretty edgy. What's the matter? . . .

If friends conscientiously perform the role-reversal exercise when the issues at hand are particularly sensitive, even though it may seem forced and silly at the beginning, many difficulties caused not by actual differences, but by misunderstanding and emotional alienation will be prevented. An argument about spending time together, for instance, might be only a symptom of two people's assumptions: "If you liked me, you'd spend more time with me" and "If you respected me, you'd trust that I like you." The fears behind the assumption are quite similar: "I'm afraid you don't like/respect me." At this level, seeming differences turn into shared experience. That is, each person might feel emotionally insecure in the relationship and the surface friction may only be an expression of the differences in the way they avoid or cope with the very similar feelings and experiences. Only by being sensitive to each other's feelings will friends achieve a level of discussion where these discoveries occur.

In addition to empathic and open communication, several guidelines for minimizing the stress of friendship are suggested:

1. *Consider compromising to resolve differences.* All friendships are rooted in reciprocity—not on a strict I-do-something-for-you-so-you-must-do-something-for-me basis, but over the length of the relationship. But what if the reciprocity breaks down and the "giving and getting" becomes an issue? Whenever differences of this nature occur, whether between friends, business partners or nations, they are resolved in one of three ways: One party attempts domination (result: hostility, war); mutual or unilateral withdrawal (result: parting, isolation); mutual compromise (result: something for something). If individuals are seeking a more satisfying relationship with each other rather than ending the friendship or suffering through interminable resentment, mutual compromise clearly offers the greatest promise.

2. *It is foolish to persistently pursue a friendship with someone who isn't interested in you.* Friendship involves a complete interplay of values and interests as well as a nonanalyzable bond between people—"chemistry" as the popular idiom has it; many people simply do not match and never will. Aside from incompatibility, some people either have other demands on their time and, literally, don't have time for you, or they are defensive,

overly shy and generally unavailable. In these instances, it is wise to accept these others as the strangers they wish to be so that you have the time and energy to invest in friendships with people who desire you.

3. *There is an oft-quoted but rarely appreciated biblical phrase:* "*Do unto others as you would have others do unto you.*" People who abide by this code are more likely to have thriving friendships. Indeed, those who are chronically unhappy with other people probably are so because of a failure to see others as similar, in many respects, to themselves. Most of us want the same things in our friendships: honesty, a sharing of feelings and thoughts, empathy, support, fun. Those of us who are not getting these qualities from others might ask: "Do I myself offer these same things to others?" There is no guarantee that being a model of what you want will produce positive results, but the probabilities increase very dramatically. How, then, do you protect the quality of a close friendship? The answer is simple. *You* attempt to move closer to your friend, you take him or her into *your* confidence and share *your* thoughts and feelings. You give what you want to get.

The Friendship Connection: Meditations

Definitions

OVER ONE HUNDRED YEARS AGO, Emerson lamented that Americans too often mistake casual acquaintances for true friends. There is even greater confusion about the meaning of friendship today. If we are to develop satisfying friendships, it is important that we have a clear notion of what we are striving for. We need to know what friendship is and what it is not. Here is a selection of historical views of friendship that can be considered along with your own.

Friendship is almost always the union of a part of one mind with a part of another; people are friends in spots.

GEORGE SANTAYANA

It appears then that genuine friendship cannot possibly exist where one of the parties is unwilling to hear the truth and the other is equally indisposed to speak it.

CICERO, 50 B.C.

Friendship is a plant of slow growth and must undergo and withstand the shocks of adversity before it is entitled to the appellation.

GEORGE WASHINGTON

A true friend is somebody who can make us do what we can.

RALPH WALDO EMERSON

Thou mayest be sure that he that will in private tell thee of thy faults, is thy friend, for he adventures thy dislike, and doth hazard thy hatred; there are few men that can endure it, every man for the most part delighting in self-praise, which is one of the most universal follies that bewitcheth mankind.

SIR WALTER RALEIGH

> A friend is one
> To whom one may pour
> Out all the contents
> Of one's heart,
> Chaff and grain together
> Knowing that the
> Gentlest of hands
> Will take and sift it,
> Keep what is worth keeping
> And with a breath of kindness
> Blow the rest away.

Arabian proverb

The test of friendship is assistance in adversity, and that too, unconditional assistance. Co-operation which needs consideration is a commercial contract and not friendship. Conditional co-operation is like adulterated cement which does not bind.

MAHATMA GANDHI

Friendship is, strictly speaking, reciprocal benevolence, which inclines each party to be solicitous for the welfare of the other as for his own. This equality of affection is created and preserved by a similarity of disposition and manners.

PLATO

Friendship is the inexpressible comfort of feeling safe with a person having neither to weigh thoughts nor measure words.

GEORGE ELIOT

Personal Musings

1.

Have you ever been refreshed, excited and later puzzled by a meeting-of-the-minds with a total stranger? Occasionally, when I've travel, this has occurred to me. A breakthrough happens, the protective armor separating us yields to unity, the most intimate revelations are exchanged. Rarely, in my experience, have these encounters resulted in a friendship. How sad. Is it the distance barrier that prevents continuance? Perhaps so. But what of those individuals in our proximity; why is friendship not pursued on the home ground? Fear. We are afraid.

Friendship is the riskiest of all investments. It is not our money, possessions, time or convenience we are putting on the line, it is ourself, our basic humanity. Fear, therefore, is the major impediment to friendship. Friendship requires that we stand naked before these others, whoever they may be, saying in effect, "This is me, I will not hide from you, I will risk being hurt." It is an invitation to put aside the mask.

2.

Masks we wear:

The Judge

The individual who feels, "I am no good," but protectively transforms this into, "*They* are no good," thus providing negative insurance in the event of a rejection: "Well, he (she) was offensive anyway!"

The Nice Guy

Exaggerates his caring; he kills with kindness. This is the chameleon who hardly ever disagrees, who convinces himself or herself to be whatever the other person in the relationship wants even though that may violate his or her integrity.

The Conqueror

Using charm, wit and flirtation, the conqueror signals his or her availability and derives great pleasure and excitement through rigorous sexual/social pursuit. As soon as the "pursued" has committed himself or herself, the conqueror's interest drops.

The Feeler

Just as some people are closed and nonexpressive, others go to the other extreme and use indiscriminate openness and the expression of what they call "genuine feelings" in the hope that this role will win them friends.

Male/Female Chauvinist

Men who take a chauvinist position are likely to whistle at, talk down to and attempt to dominate women. Women are likely to feel *consistently* sexualized, to be humorless and constantly to challenge even the slightest hint of unfairness in their male acquaintances. At base, both men and women who hold to these rigid positions are afraid of each other.

Whether an individual masquerades in one of these false faces or chooses another—that of the suffering stoic, the wounded idealist, the witty comic, the innocent victim or the rueful sinner —doesn't matter. Whether people conceal themselves in this manner or behind business banter, name dropping or business talk, the result is the same. All fictitious façades—cover-ups for the fear that we are unworthy as we are—defeat the possibility of a lasting friendship.

3.

A friendship in which each tries to control the other is doomed. The situation is reminiscent of two sailors hanging out of either side of a sailboat in order to steady it; the more one leans overboard in an effort to control the craft, the more the other has to hang out to compensate for the instability created by the other's attempts at control, while the boat itself would be quite steady if not for the insecurities of its passengers. It is predictable that unless each lets go, allows the other "to be," the occupants of the friendship boat will be under constant unnecessary strain and, worse yet, finish up in the sea of loneliness.

4.

Husband: I think I'd like to get in touch with my buddy Harold.

Wife: What do you want with him? He's such a boozer!

Husband: Maybe I'll give Murray a call.

Wife: Murray! After the way he snubbed you on your birthday?

Husband: Jeff, now there's a real friend. We've known each other since childhood.

Wife: How could you continue a relationship with him? He's gay. You two live in different worlds.

Husband: I know, I'll drop in on Larry, he's a real pal.

Wife: Some pal, he's owed you thirty dollars for the last four years.

Husband: You know, hon, I was just thinking. I don't have a friend left whom I knew before I married you.

Wife: Don't worry, dear, you don't need them; I'm your friend.

How many married couples do you know who freely allow each other individual friends outside the marriage? Probably very few. Most couples insulate themselves and, in time, use each other up. Togetherness carried to extremes results in isolation.

5.

What is a friend? The answer, given as a conditioned response, is most often: "One who will be there in troubled times." Having someone there to hold your hand when it feels as if the world has done you in seems to be universally valued. But friendship is more than crisis sharing. Many of us, myself included, hunger not for a lifesaver; we are searching for fellow travelers, companions of our inner life who share our ecstasies, dreams and fears. Friendship of this sort is born when, after disclosing a secret evil or hidden hope, we hear the statement "What! You too? I thought I was the only one. . . ."

6.

I had a friend once whose approval I sought and so each time we met I tried to impress him with my latest accomplishments: "Did you see my article in *New Woman*? Doing national TV sure is exciting!" But the more I lauded my success the less inclined he was to spend time with me. It wasn't until the original fire of our friendship was thoroughly banked that I finally realized how hard I had made it for him to feel good about himself. I regret my insensitivity and am embarrassed to think that it never dawned on me to consider his needs as well as mine. For he suffered from the same "look at me, aren't I terrific" malady as I.

7.

If two people do not exist as separate individuals, then their friendship is an illusion.

In the dance of friendship, so much of what you see depends on where you are standing when you look. In newly formed friendships we see only the other's virtues. At some latter point, perhaps when inflated expectations have left open wounds, there is a tendency to see only faults. If a relationship survives this critical moment there is the possibility of capturing the other's complexity and becoming true friends.

The social butterflies of our society collect people and thereby avoid closeness: The more people they surround themselves with, the less chance there is of establishing relationships that are of emotional consequence. Spreading themselves thin provides justification for not spreading themselves thick.

8.

There are people who make good acquaintances and bad friends. Al is such a person. An engaging, gregarious, very bright fellow, he has a large social network. Al is forever developing new business schemes, dreaming up elaborate plans and projects involving other people. On several occasions I have approached Al and he has enthusiastically agreed to get together for a social evening. My intent was to get to know him better, to develop a friendship. The problem is that Al invariably cancels our meeting for another appointment, forgets about our meeting or, as sometimes happens, he shows up hours late apologizing profusely: "Oh, I'm terribly sorry, something came up."

At first I thought maybe it was me, but after listening to several acquaintances we have in common voice similar complaints, I became curious. "Al, what's with you," I asked one day. "Why do you overcommit yourself like that?" After a brief conversation the answer was clear: Al is one of those people who think you have to be all things to all people in order to be liked. What he doesn't seem to realize is that if he isn't true to someone, if there isn't someone he refuses to masquerade in front of, then his life is going to be a succession of discovered deceits. Because he is so clever, so charming, he thinks any understanding friend would forgive him. But he will not be forgiven. Al will remain an acquaintance, not a friend.

9.

Feelings are the connective tissue of friendship. Without the exchange of feelings, a relationship is likely to wither, to turn into the muted boredom of the habitual. Yet, for all the lip service we pay to the expression of feelings, most of us rarely take our emotional temperature—at least not publicly. Our restraint starts in childhood when we are told by our elders to keep our mouths shut and hide our feelings. Later, when we go to school we learn about math, geography and grammar, but feelings are left out of the curriculum. As adults, we are busy; we have goals to reach, achievements to attain, and days pass quickly without much attention to feelings. Your job may be in jeopardy, one of your children may be sick, and you may have a cold coming on—but if a friend asks in passing how you feel, you will probably reply, "I'm fine." This kind of superficial exchange is merely a sign of friendliness, not an expression of feelings. Life is full of such rituals—harmless small talk. The trouble is that over the years these shallow, habitual responses become so ingrained that we devalue the importance of our own feelings and those of the significant people in our lives; we lose touch with the stuff of which friendships are made.

10.

Old patterns die hard. Despite the campaign against rigid sexual roles waged by the various liberation movements, it can hardly be said that the majority of men and women see beyond being partners in bed. Not long ago I had two colleagues, Sheri and Michael, who really enjoyed each other's company but who typified the cross-sex friendship dilemma. Both were in reasonably solid marriages and neither held a strong sexual attraction for the other. Michael yearned to spend time outside the office with Sheri but was afraid his wife would get the wrong impression and also feared offending Sheri by not coming on to her sexually. Sheri shared a similar wish for Michael's companionship; she would have liked to have had dinner with him but worried what her husband would think and was equally restrained by her assumption that Michael would consider her too forward and expect sex as part of the arrangement. Neither Sheri nor Michael breached their sex stereotypes, and eventually they went their separate ways leaving friendship, an undeveloped resource, behind.

11.

The German philosopher Schopenhauer told the story of two porcupines huddled together on a cold winter's night. The temperature dropped; the animals moved closer together. But then there was a problem; each kept getting "stuck" by the other's quills. Finally, with much shifting and shuffling in changing positions, they managed to work out an equilibrium whereby each got maximum warmth with a minimum of painful pricking from the other.

Friends have something in common with the huddling porcupines. They want to achieve and maintain a kind of equilibrium; warmth and intimacy but without the continuous "pricking" that can become agonizing in a close relationship. The attainment of this proper distance is what creates the "gusto" of a healthy friendship. Such a distance, though, does not imply a conflict-free stance; rather, it is a position which allows one friend to withstand and where necessary even to pierce the other.

12.

A friend called me recently to tell me of a problem he was having. I listened. We talked it out together. Later he called back to thank me and tell me how much lighter he felt. I may as well have thanked him in return; after our conversation I noticed my own ailments had also been lifted. The pattern is not new; whenever I connect with another human being it recurs.

We live in a society in which many people purchase friendship by the hour from those in the psychological professions. The time has come for us to recognize the loving potential each of us holds, to reach out for each other and befriend rather than alienate one another.

Speaking of Friendships: Philosophers and Kindred Souls

Social scientists, for the most part, have steered clear of the friendship experience. One reason for the lack of scientific scrutiny is obvious to anyone who has been involved in a friendship

—it is one of the most difficult of human enterprises. Nonetheless, philosophers and their soulmates—poets and mystics—have dared enter where scientists fear to tread. Some of their thoughts follow.

Be slow to fall into friendship; but when thou art in, continue firm and constant.

SOCRATES

The only way to have a friend is to be one.

EMERSON

> There is no friend like an old friend
> Who has shared our morning days.
> No greeting like his welcome,
> No homage like his praise.

OLIVER WENDELL HOLMES

There are three friendships which are advantageous: friendship with the upright, with the sincere and with the man of much observation. Friendship with the man of specious airs, with the insinuatingly soft, and with the glib-tongued, these are injurious.

CONFUCIUS

The most I can do for my friend is simply to be his friend.

HENRY DAVID THOREAU

In poverty and other misfortunes of life, true friends are a sure refuge. The young they keep out of mischief; to the old they are a comfort and aid in their weakness, and those in the prime of life they incite to noble deeds.

ARISTOTLE

A principal fruit of friendship is the ease and discharge of the fullness of the heart, which passions of all kinds do cause and induce. The diseases of stoppings and suffocations are the most dangerous in the body; and it is not much otherwise in the mind; you may take sorza to open the liver, steel to open the spleen, flower of sulphur for the lungs, castoreum for the brain, but no receipt openeth the heart but a true friend, to whom you may impart griefs, joys, fears, hopes, suspicions, counsels, and whatsoever lieth upon the heart to oppress it, in a kind of civil shift or confession.

FRANCIS BACON

The better part of one's life consists of his friendships.

ABRAHAM LINCOLN

With respect to your friends, I would wish you to choose them neither from caprice nor accident, and to adhere to them as long as you can. Do not make a surfeit of friendship, through over sanguine enthusiasm, nor expect it to last forever. Always speak well of those with whom you have once been intimate, or take some part of the censure you bestow on them to yourself. Never quarrel with tried friends, or those whom you wish to continue such. When once the prejudice is removed that sheathes defects, familiarity only causes jealousy and distrust. Do not keep on with a mockery of friendship after the substance is gone—but part, while you can part friends. Bury the carcass of friendship: It is not worth embalming.

WILLIAM HAZLITT

The costliness of keeping friends does not lie in what one does for them but in what one, out of consideration for them, refrains from doing.

HENRIK IBSEN

> Don't walk in front of me
> I may not follow
> Don't walk behind me
> I may not lead
> Walk beside me
> And just be my friend.

ALBERT CAMUS

Two men were traveling in company through a forest, when all at once, a huge bear crashed out of the brush near them. One of the men, thinking of his own safety, climbed a tree. The other, unable to fight the savage beast alone, threw himself on the ground and lay still, as if he were dead. He had heard that a bear will not touch a dead body.

It must have been true, for the bear sniffed at the man's head a while, and then, seeming to be satisfied that he was dead, walked away.

The man in the tree climbed down.

"It looked as if that bear whispered something in your ear," he said. "What did he tell you?"

"He said," answered the other, "that it was not at all wise to keep company with a fellow who would desert his friend in a moment of danger."

AESOP'S FABLES

You can choose your friends but you can't choose your relatives.

CHARLIE BROWN

Journey's End: Highlights and Implications

A REAL FRIENDSHIP—as anyone who has ever had one can attest—is as difficult to describe as it is to develop. Friend, as we have seen, can be a word more emotion packed and embracing than husband, wife, lover, sister or brother. A paraplegic veteran, inconsolable, says of his buddy killed in Vietnam: "We were not just fellow victims of the war, you see. He was my best friend. I loved him more than my own brother." A woman sitting with her lover turns to him and declares, "You are the first man I count as my friend. That means more to me than anything I've experienced with a man." Speaking of his wife a man remarks, "We've shared our bed, our home, our lives for thirty years." Then, choked with emotion, he refers to her as his "treasured friend." Friendship can be larger than other relations or, sadly, it may not be a part of them. While the term is used to describe the people one loves most in life, it is also used to describe an acquaintance with whom one has nothing in common but temporary proximity. A catchword, friend.

The meaning of friendship can be as tangled and mysterious as that of love; the experiences of over two thousand people, generously shared, confirm it to be as with love affairs, one of the most pleasurable and most difficult of specifically human activities. The survey findings have touched on a good many issues related to the central theme of friendship. Survey respondents have discussed the benefits as well as the frustrations to be found in friendship. We have considered the conditions that give rise to friendship, the "feel" of friendship and the ways individuals manage their friendships. We have looked at the influence of competition, success, fame and romantic love. From these findings a diverse and sometimes surprising picture of friendship in America has emerged. Here are the highlights:

The experience of friendship with someone—family member or non-blood related—is not a mere luxury. For optimal functioning it is an imperative. Consider childhood. These early friendships, as psychologist Harry F. Harlow in a famous study demonstrated, are vital for a child's social development. Professor Harlow raised a group of baby monkeys, the primates closest to humans, with cloth surrogate mothers, another group with unaffectionate mothers and a third group with no mothers at all. Those monkeys allowed to form affectional relationships with peers initially showed some social maladjustment but eventually improved and functioned adequately. Baby monkeys deprived of adequate mothering and of contact with peers for about six months became social isolates with enduring socialization problems.

Although my survey was not designed to uncover the impact of childhood friendships on later life, a review of the clinical literature supports Dr. Harlow's observations. There is no question among authorities on child development that friendless children are higher risks for emotional disturbances. Childhood friends are the first link with the world outside our family. They help us begin the process of separation from our parents; they teach us by their reactions acceptable social behavior; through friends we become introduced to the world of sex, and friends as well as parents contribute to our moral development.

The rich opportunities for self-exploration and personality expansion that can be a part of the early friendship experience were described to me by an energetic sixty-three-year-old grandfather. While watching his grandchildren play with their friends he began to think about his own childhood friendships:

"One of the things that I couldn't understand as a child was how I seemed to change my personality when playing with different friends. Admittedly, I was quite overprotected and on the goody-goody side. But this quality was exaggerated significantly when I played with Daryl Mazen. He had the reputation in our quiet, sedate Italian/Jewish neighborhood of being a real terror. He was ill tempered, outspoken to the point of being rude to adults (which was shocking in those days) and was a behavior problem in school. As I recall, he was left back—although he was very bright. Most of the other children were frightened of Daryl and I think he became fiercely loyal to me, if for no other reason than my willingness to play with him at all.

"As good and proper as I was, my friendship with Daryl allowed me to become—in my imagination at the very least—just a shade bolder, which I think was needed. With Daryl I learned to roller skate (and get up quickly when I fell), build things (usually from 'borrowed' parts) and to pamper myself less. But when I played with Mitchell, who was even more timid than I, I felt the way Daryl must have with me: I was protective of him. I kept a lid on my language and behavior so as not to shock Mitchell. Even though he was a few months older than I, he was like a kid brother to me. Just as Daryl helped me moderate the overly proper aspect of myself, my friendship with Mitchell stretched me further. With him I could have a taste of the excitement of being tough, protective and in charge without having to take any great risks."

With the rapid growth and change of youngsters, early friendships, predictably, are not marked by constancy. Although most survey respondents recall a close special friend during their teen and preteen years, many reported being in and out of friendships frequently. At age eight Susan has a need to be big sister to her friends, just as her older sister lords it over her. A month later, a year later, Susan no longer feels the need to dominate; now the big attraction is to find a friend who shares her interest in music. Harvey, a shy youngster, may seek out a quiet, genteel friend; some other time, having outgrown his shyness, Harvey may find an outgoing, even rebellious youngster a more appealing friend. We desire friends, yes—but our desires change and can create a gap between ourselves and our friends. This is a universal dilemma in our fast-paced society and not easily resolved at any point in the life cycle.

Friendship is a sensitive arrangement for all of us; it often does not proceed smoothly. For women, though, it has been lauded as a near-impossible achievement. There are no myths of devoted women friends comparable to David and Jonathan, Achilles and Patroclus, Damon and Pythias, all of whom are memorialized by virtue of their friendship. Sappho and her friends, in contrast, have been relegated to the discounted category of lesbianism. Through both printed and film media, women learn of their inability to bond, their competition over men; they are depicted as "bitchy," "catty" to one another. Yes, there are elements of truth in these accusations. Witness women angry with each other over the Equal Rights Amendment; the competition in motherhood . . . "my son the doctor"; the last-minute rejection of a friend in favor of a date, "Oh, Jane, do you mind? . . ." But according to the survey responses, the popular characterization of female friendship is oversimplified and distorted.

To start with, unlike men, who tend to have a kind of "I made it and I have no affiliation with anyone who hasn't. . . . I have no feeling at all for a person who can't get it together and be where I am" attitude, many women provide enormous support systems for one another. Women have also become increasingly aware and increasingly inclined to reject the stereotypes that have been imposed on them. This is partly due to the women's movement and to greater self-confidence; but also, as women have gained and employed more options in their lives, they are making female friends beyond those made in childhood or school, beyond those in their children's play groups or in car pools. With more women in the work force, they are no longer exclusively confined to domestic dialogue and consequently have developed broader connections with each other.

Friendship involves a commitment to and interest in another person's welfare. In turn, this demands that one trust another to keep that commitment. Can people attain that trust in one another? The survey results indicate that for many women, particularly in their thirties—after their career strivings and family obligations have taken manageable form—the answer is affirmative. For men—most of whom have grown up with an idealized picture of friendship—the answer is distinctly less positive. The fact is that trust is a rare commodity among men.

A young woman recently arrived in New York was invited to a small gathering by her new neighbor. At one point in the evening she found herself alone with an older woman. The older woman spoke of her work, her fear of losing her position to a younger, more energetic woman. And the younger woman, who felt stagnant and restless in her job, empathized and unselfconsciously told of her own plight. Although these two women could easily have become adversaries in a discussion which touched a vulnerable spot in them both—the older one felt insecure and the younger one hungry—they did not. Rather, by the time they were joined by other guests they were plunged into a deep, intimate conversation. It is difficult to imagine two men becoming so quickly intimate about so sensitive a subject.

Survey results posit an unwillingness among men to disclose vulnerabilities for fear they will be used against them. Men fear that if they tell another man that they are insecure about the kind of work they are doing, the guy will try for the job; they are reluctant to talk about their love relations (other than to boast of their victories), for fear another man will move in on them. And worse, men fear fear itself most of all. To acknowledge insecurity, loneliness, to say "I am scared," is to lose face and be considered unmanly. Men can be harsh judges of one another. Being so frightened of anything considered weak, men are often unsettled by self-disclosure—their own as well as their fellow's. It is as if weakness in one man suggests—horror of horrors—that all men are vulnerable.

Men have come down from the trees and out of the caves and perhaps even ventured out into the community but they still wield a club to those they fear—their fellow man. Friendship requires a laying down of arms; it is a surrender in which the fortress that men build to separate themselves from others is disassembled. Some men have done this; they have conquered their fear. They are a minority; although all males are influenced by cultural values imploring them to be ruggedly invulnerable and unyieldingly competitive, not all men are unthinking puppets adhering to these constricting stereotypes. Some men told of experiences with other men which have had a profound effect on their personal lives. Whether it's a next-door neighbor, a co-worker or a golf partner, it appears that men are slowly beginning to increase their connection with each other in important ways. Male camaraderie may be scarce, but the trend—particularly among those who were in high school and college during the turbulent sixties and are now in their thirties—is on the upswing.

Men and women, because of the differences worked by environment, conditioning and differing expectations, do not often form friendships with each other. It is possible, even probable, that as men and women occupy more approximate occupational positions and view their differences with less acrimony, cross-sex friendships will improve. As for the sexual dimension, we are, undeniably, sexual beings—very few of us approach others as absolute neuters—and it is unrealistic to expect sexuality to go underground in cross-sex friendships. Unfortunately, with sexual intimacy often come jealousy and possessiveness: Which is why strong sexual attraction and friendship are a very difficult course to navigate. It is a relatively rare occurrence for a sexual relationship (outside of marriage or other committed arrangements) to coexist with friendship; and it is a frustrating experience to form a close relationship with someone where sexual attraction is rampant yet unfulfilled. The survey data suggest that cross-sex friendships (with someone other than one's mate) work best when the sexual attraction is low or both individuals are romantically committed elsewhere.

Disillusioned with cross-sex friendships not bound by marriage, some people look to their marital vows with the hope that they have found a friend forever. Modern marriage has been described as one of the saviors of western civilization; it offers a unique combination of romantic passion, loving friendship and economic partnership. The satisfaction of romantic passion and economic partnership is left for other investigations. As for loving friendship, again the myth was found to be mightier than the reality. Less than one-third of married respondents regarded their mates as friends!

In addition to pointing up a need for better marital preparation—perhaps incorporating into school curricula instructional material on interpersonal relationships, personal communication skills and shared parenting roles—these findings warn against the extreme demand for marital togetherness sanctioned by our society. Instead of a code for bonding, most of us have been indoctrinated with one of bondage. Like Siamese twins, we must always appear as a couple. No other society, to my knowledge, expects as much from marriage—the source of all emotional satisfaction—as ours. As a means of attaining fulfillment for two individuals, the institution of marriage has imperfections and limitations. Many marriages don't work or they don't work for very long. It is likely that a goodly percentage collapse from mere overload. Most of us are aware of this—we acknowledge that even at its best, marriage cannot meet all the needs of both spouses all the time. In practice, though, we frequently ignore this fundamental truth. How many couples in our society freely allow each other strong individual friendships outside marriage? Very few indeed.

When a married person does develop an individual friendship outside of coupledom, it is least likely to be with someone who is unmarried. It is evident from the survey results that we are well on the way to developing two distinct kinds of social life, each of which categorically excludes a large segment of the population. Most married couples seek out other couples exclusively and, if they develop an individual friendship, it is usually with one half of the couple—predictably, the same-sex half. At social gatherings, there is likely to be an even number of men and women with no extras—no unattached men or women—to complicate the situation.

The net result of this exclusivity—one way of living for marrieds bringing up children and another way for singles—is loss. For those who are married, family life becomes increasingly narrow and humdrum; singles, in contrast, miss exposure to families which can potentially contribute to a sense of wholeness in their lives. Children, too, benefit by an assortment of different types of people in their lives. A married couple who socialize with unmarried friends of different ages, both sexes and varied interests offer their youngsters an opportunity to increase their knowledge of life styles and of people generally.

If divorce strikes—as it does in almost four out of ten marriages —both husbands and wives who have restricted each other's friendship choices are unlikely to escape with impunity. Both become, by this event, threatened with agonizing loneliness. As with other high-risk loneliness groups—the elderly, the highly mobile and the widowed—the married person who separates from a spouse is suddenly faced with a loss of relationships due to sharply changed circumstances. It is at this time that the fabric of extramarital friendship is tested; often relationships developed in marriage prove to be thinly based and fragile.

When the dissolution of a marriage highlights the superficiality of social relations, men often turn to work for diversion; those women who are primarily homemakers are most apt to enter into more active involvement with their children. Even men who are not preoccupied with success may, in an effort to anesthetize themselves, experience a temporary burst of ambition in which they seek overtime and bring work home. Despite these efforts on the part of both men and women, they remain lonely. People without emotional attachment cannot escape loneliness through activity. There is no substitute for the absence of relationship. Compensations do not remedy deficits; they are useful only as palliatives until the real thing can be attained. Divorce harshly reminds us that friendship is not just an "extra" to be indulged in, in order to brighten up life; it is a critical source of emotional satisfaction.

The picture is not entirely grim. For one thing, although most of the separated lose access to their network of married friends, some remain in touch with one or two couples and may even become closer to them than they had been previously. Further, the great majority of those divorced eventually develop a new network of friends. Some not only recoup their losses but, having learned the value of friendship, develop a richer social life and closer friends than they had when they were married.

In contrast to the divorce experience, of interest mainly to those who have been or fear being touched by it, Americans from all walks of life seem to be tireless in their fascination with fame. We are of mixed mind when it comes to celebrity status— at once we envy the famous for their popularity and suspect that underneath it all, they are unbearably lonely. In a recent issue of *Esquire* magazine, several famous people were asked about their friendships. Their reactions led to this statement from *Esquire* reporters: "It came as no surprise when a number of celebrities invited to appear in our pages with their best and trusted friends suddenly remembered they had a plane to catch. Famous people always seem to find it easier to have a million friends than one good friend...."

This may be so with some celebrities, but it is also true of noncelebrities. And this is the point: From the celebrities I spoke to, the friendship experience is not dramatically altered by notoriety. Sure, celebrities are more protective of their time. But they must be; more is demanded of them. More fundamentally, they share with the rest of humanity a need for relationships characterized by authenticity, acceptance and understanding. They, like us, suffer in the absence of these psychological nutrients and prosper in their presence.

For all of us, the friendship journey can be a voyage of discovery. Unlike the more institutional relations of kin, friendships are not subject to a ready "job description." Lacking societal ground rules or legal validation, friendship alliances are fascinating but they are also filled with paradox, contradictions and exceptions. With freedom of choice comes greater complexity; there is no magic formula for friendship that fits us all. The implications of the friendship experience, being so complex, are far from completely known. An easily applied set of guidelines does not exist; there are too many exceptions and too much relativity. Some general observations, however, do apply.

1. Friendships are traditionally supposed to survive, as with family ties, throughout the lifetimes of the people involved. Our culture places high value on "old friends," and a certain amount of shame is associated with dropping a long-standing friendship. Although long-time friendships are comforting, we might as well get used to the fact that with our increasing mobility and rising rates of occupational turnover, temporary relationships are here to stay. John Barth, in a passage from his novel *The Floating Opera*, captures the trend: "Our friends float past; we become involved with them; they float on, and we must rely on hearsay or lose

track of them completely; they float back again, and we must either renew our friendship—catch up to date—or find that they and we don't comprehend each other any more."

This is no small or easy matter. It accounts, in part, for the much-lamented "loss of commitment" that is characteristic of our time. As people shift from job to job, from location to location, they are conditioned to guard themselves against the pain of disaffiliation. They learn to armor themselves against a sad goodbye by not laying much of their heart on the line. Those people who are less adept at the business of coping with temporary relationships—those who take longer to establish ties and who are reluctant to let them go—have the hardest time of it. Thus, we may see larger numbers of people living closer to and depending more on their relatives than on friends. This suggests, as Alvin Toffler found in his book *Future Shock*, that if friendship, along with family, is to remain a prominent feature in our lives, we need to develop our abilities not only in initiating relationships but in ending them; we need to learn not only to affiliate but to disaffiliate.

2. Related to the issue discussed above is our attitude toward temporary relationships. Those of us raised on the notion that friendship is for the long haul believe that stable and enduring relationships are the only ones in which we can have commitment. Short-term and temporary relationships are considered necessarily superficial. Long-term relationships do offer a kind of anchoring and an opportunity for development that is unique, but the assumption that temporary relationships *must* be devoid of commitment needs to be reconsidered. There are other dimensions to commitment besides time. Despite the brief longevity of the friendship, you can be committed to respecting the integrity of the other person and the authenticity of your response. You can be committed to being without artifice and without pretension. Just as enduring friendships are valued, briefer relationships are an opportunity to concentrate on what we have to share in that short time without the impedimenta of past experiences or the problems of the future.

3. The prevailing view of American cities colors them as cold and dispassionate, while small towns are described as places where

everyone knows each other, where stability and commitment and a strong sense of belonging reign supreme. Is friendship a lost art to the urbanite? Not so. To the contrary, I found for the city dweller—both men and women expressed greater friendship satisfaction than the small town or rural inhabitant.

This finding—that small towns are not necessarily fertile breeding grounds for friendship—was first pointed out in the mid-1920s. A team of researchers interviewed a sample of residents of Muncie, Indiana, then a town of under 50,000, and found that one-third of the working-class wives and one out of eight of the businessmen's wives had no intimate friends at all in town. "We've let all our friends slip away as our children have taken up more and more of our time," explained one of the women. Even those women who talked about having friends expressed dissatisfaction: "I don't see my friends at all," said one woman. "That is really true—I never see them unless I run into them occasionally...."

Over a decade later, the researchers returned to Muncie for a follow-up study. What they found was more of the same. If anything, people felt even more isolated. Looking for a friend? It seems you are more likely to be successful searching among the concrete structures than among the trees of small-town America.

4. We select our friends out of a very large pool of acquaintanceships. In a study conducted by Michael Gurevitch at the Massachusetts Institute of Technology, researchers asked a varied group of individuals to keep track of all the different people with whom they come in contact in a 100-day period. On average, each person listed some 500 names. Social psychologist Stanley Milgram, who cites the Gurevitch study in a *Psychology Today* article and who has conducted a number of experiments dealing with communication through acquaintanceship networks, has found similarly that the average American has anywhere from 500 to 2,500 acquaintances and associations. From these hundreds of people, however, we choose few real friends.

On what basis is the friendship choice made? How do we sort a friend out of a large pool of acquaintances? It is easy enough to say that friendships are likely to be built around common interests and values. But that isn't enough to fully explain close relationships. Many of our acquaintances have similar interests and values compatible with our own, yet we form strong ties with only a few of them. We can list the appealing qualities of friendship—openness, trust, good humor, sensitivity and the like—but we probably have acquaintances with many of these same qualities who fail to ignite in us the spark of interest, the loyalty of close attachment. And some of our closest friends have some very irritating qualities. There seems to be no satisfactory answer. Like religion, friendship demands an initial leap of faith or daring that may be developed or eventually disavowed. Beyond social class and age factors, which virtually every study, including this one, affirms to be important—the reasons why two people join in friendship cannot be fully accounted for; the basis for friendship choices remains a mystery.

5. Those people who are plagued with loneliness and depression would be wise to note that these are often not merely "personal" problems but are interpersonal issues. In our search for the source of unhappy states it is time that we go beyond the deep recesses of the unconscious and explore the nature of our relations with others. "I've gone through different brands of therapy and run the gamut of encounter groups, but none of them taught me how to become close to people, how to make friends," one man told me. Friendship is not usually in the foreground of a psychotherapy patient's complaints, yet it can be seen to be looming pervasively in the background. And after years of therapy when a person's life constellation has been thoroughly explored, it is often the case that the friendship experience should have been a focal point from the beginning.

One researcher has even noted that some young preschizophrenic youngsters can be protected from deteriorating by a close friendship. And in the massive Midtown Manhattan study of 1954, involving 1,660 men, women and children, the association between friendship and mental health was supported. A very high risk of poor mental health was found in friendless individuals. Interestingly, the number of acquaintances the individuals had was only moderately associated with sound functioning. Friendship played a much more important role. My investigation updates and confirms this aspect of the Midtown Manhattan study. Consistently, those individuals reporting satisfactory friendship (but not so for looser associations) complained less often of depression and loneliness than their friendless counterparts.

Is there one grand conclusion to be drawn from all this? Hardly. There is, however, an important trend to report: Many of us are at war with our fellows. Some, damaged by the psychological battles they wage, have withdrawn completely. Others preach self-love, separateness, independence, doing your own thing. "Me" reigns as the new God. We have gone from Barbra Streisand's *People Who Need People* to Paul Simon's *Fifty Ways to Leave Your Lover*. The new narcissism is evident in the proliferation of therapies that declare we should be our own best friends, devote ourselves to self-growth and self-actualization, and look out, above all, for "No. 1." As a result our society, particularly in the last decade, has been out of balance, with too much emphasis on self and not nearly enough appreciation for the equally necessary and different struggle for union.

We are slowly moving from a mood of self-absorption to issues involving other people. There is beginning to emerge a renewed appreciation for intimacy and interpersonal relationships. This comes at a time when families are much more fragmented than they used to be, when vast numbers of people have become uprooted from their birthplaces, and society is changing more rapidly than ever. Yet despite these obstacles, the desire for friendship glimmers as if to testify to its resilience. Can it be that the "Me" decade is fading, giving way to an era where "We" is gaining in prominence?

Let's hope so. Although the best preparation for union is independence, taken to the extreme, independence is nothing more than another defense, a protection against the fear of being hurt. Our retreat to separateness may be lined with all the signposts of personal glory—position, prestige, accomplishment—but can glory offer a warm embrace? Can we entrust our dreams and fears to prestige? Will accomplishment listen as we speak the unspeakable? Will position accept our faults? Of course not. Individual growth is nurtured by relationships; growth ceases when it is steadfastly put first. No, the answer doesn't lie in the protection of separateness—it lies in learning how to go forth despite periods of betrayal and disappointment. The more we reach out to other people, the more life we bring to each other; the person who has no sister or brother by amity is lacking part of a family.

Bibliography

Barth, John. *The Floating Opera*. New York: Avon Books, 1956.

Block, Joel D. *The Other Man, The Other Woman*. New York: Grosset & Dunlap, 1978.

Block, Joel D. *To Marry Again*. New York: Grosset & Dunlap, 1979.

Booth, Alan. "Sex and Social Participation." *American Sociological Review* 37 (1972):183–92.

Brain, Robert. *Friends and Lovers*. New York: Basic Books, 1976.

Harlow, H. F., and Harlow, M. "Learning to Love." *American Scientist* 54, 3 (1966):190–201.

Hartley, Ruth. "Sex Role Pressure in the Socialization of the Male Child." *Psychological Reports* 5 (1959):458–62.

Jourard, Sidney M. *The Transparent Self*. New York: Van Nostrand Reinhold, 1971.

Komarovsky, Mirra. *Blue Collar Marriage*. New York: Random House, 1962.

Lucas, Rex A. *Men in Crisis*. New York: Basic Books, 1970.

Lynd, R. S., and Lynd, H. M. *Middletown in Transition*. New York: Harcourt, Brace and World, 1937.

Mead, Margaret. *Male and Female*. New York: Morrow, 1949.

Milgram, Stanley. "The Small World Problem." *Psychology Today* (May 1967):61–67.

Nelson, Linden L., and Kagan, Spencer. "Competition: The Star-Spangled Scramble." *Psychology Today* (September 1972): 53–91.

Santayana, George. *Little Essays*. Edited by L. P. Smith. London, 1920.

Toffler, Alvin. *Future Shock*. New York: Random House, 1970.

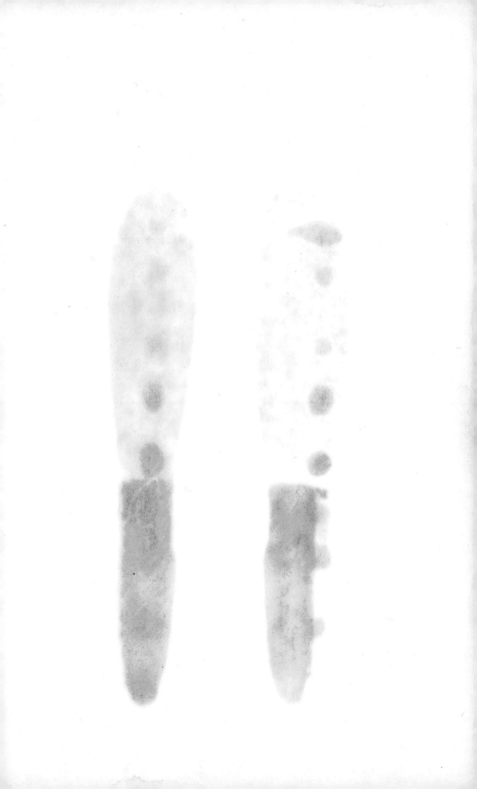

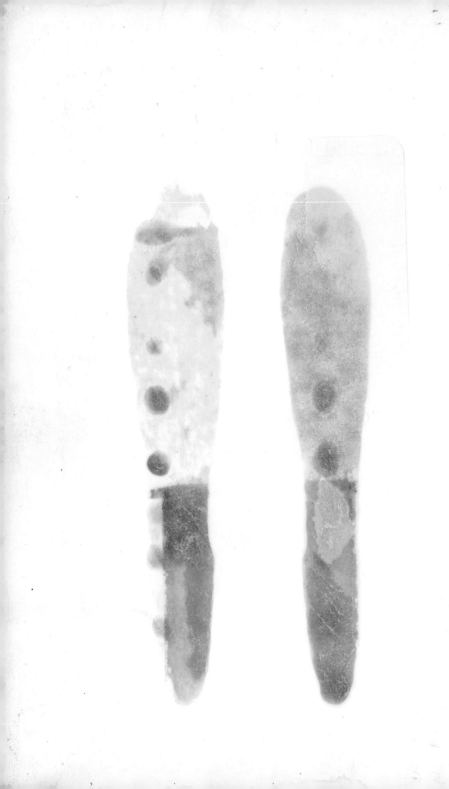